Perfect Phrases
for Classroom Teachers

Perfect Phrases
for Classroom Teachers

Hundreds of Ready-to-Use Phrases
for Parent-Teacher Conferences, Report Cards,
IEPs, and Other School Documents

Christine Canning Wilson

New York   Chicago   San Francisco   Lisbon   London   Madrid   Mexico City
Milan   New Delhi   San Juan   Seoul   Singapore   Sydney   Toronto

The *McGraw·Hill* Companies

9 10 11 12 13 14 15 16   QFR   21 20 19 18 17

ISBN   978-0-07-163015-3
MHID   0-07-163015-5

e-ISBN 978-0-07-163334-5
e-MHID   0-07-163334-0

Library of Congress Cataloging-in-Publication Data

Wilson, Christine Canning.
    Perfect phrases for classroom teachers : hundreds of ready-to-use phrases
  for parent-teacher conferences, report cards, IEPs, and other school documents /
  Christine Canning Wilson.
        p.   cm.
      ISBN 0-07-163015-5 (alk. paper)
      1. Communication in education.   2. Teacher effectiveness.   3. Teaching—
  Terminology.   I. Title.

  LB1033.5.W55   2008
  371.3—dc22   2009012425

McGraw-Hill books are available at special quantity discounts to use as premiums and sales promotions, or for use in corporate training programs. To contact a representative, please e-mail us at bulksales@mcgraw-hill.com.

Contents

Contents

Preface

First, thank you for investing in yourself as a teacher, administrator, or educator of children by purchasing this book. This book was designed to aid the classroom teacher and to meet the needs of school districts. As a previous language specialist and public speaker contracted with the U.S. Department of State, and as an award-winning educational consultant who has worked in elementary, secondary, and higher education with districts, ministries of education, and industries worldwide, I am aware of the discrepancies in our field. This book was written to help you create a baseline to become the best teaching professional you can be.

In my years of experience, I have learned that the key to gaining people's empathy, sympathy, and attention is effectively drawing them into your world. Each word you use must be exact to avoid turning a minor situation into a major lawsuit. Like a puppet master, you must serve as the controller of information. That information is released in oral or written form. The process may seem like common sense, but it is, in fact, a valued art form.

This book will teach you guidelines for phrasing information in a manner that will give you the best results. As an expert in the area of English as a second language, I have studied how intonation, syntax, paralinguistic cues, and many other factors affect second-language acquisition. Many of the universal concepts used in linguistics also apply to the world of business, industry, and, especially, education, because they dictate how we communicate information. The phrases suggested in this book are adaptable to many educational situations. By buying this reference book, you have invested in your career.

Warm regards and all the best to you in your teaching career.

Acknowledgments

I would like to first thank my McGraw-Hill editor, Kathryn Keil, whose guidance was much appreciated; also, a special thanks to project editor Craig Bolt. I would like to further thank my children, Katherine and Alexander Wilson, and my late husband, Douglas, who are my world. In addition, I would like to thank Kathleen Canning-Bubniak and John Canning; Maria Ouelette-Canning; Greg Bubniak; and Eina, Jillian, and David Wilson. Thanks also go to my in-laws Sarah and Alex. But a special thanks, if not a heartfelt dedication, goes to my very supportive parents (who are both former teachers and administrators), John and Kathleen Canning, of Pittsfield, Massachusetts, who have helped me every step of the way!

I would like to dedicate this book to the people who inspire me with their friendship and guidance: Dr. Leah Bornstein-Findley; Dr. Lisa Barlow; Dr. Linda Day; Dr. Christine Coombe; Geoff Stout; Dr. Salah Troudi; Judy and Michelle Williamson; Laura Vance; Casey Malarcher; Sue Powell; George Peknik; Cecilia Kawar; Lily Ford; Macarena Aguilar; Elliott Dreger; Marlys Berg; Anthony Antil; Dawn and Amber Kotski-Hertzberg; Lou Reilly; Johnny, John, and Rosey McLaughlin; Justin Miaa; Judy Fairweather and Paul Perry; Nancy Woitkowski; Greg Selah; Katie Shawn Kerwood; Kim Senger; Margaret Coyne; Kathleen, Ed, Steve, Karen, Michael, John, and Kevin Kotski; Denise, David, and Eleanor Withers; Thomas and Linzie Simpson; Kellie and Jeff Montleone; Louise Brogran; Michael, Marylou, and Bob Galliher; Joyce Culverwell, SSJ; Lil Quinn; Barbara Faille and Kathryn Flanagan, SSJ; Fr. Peter Gregory; Fr.

Michael Shavonvich; Margaret Downing; Dr. Joe Berger; Ibrahim Ali; Yousef Al Jabri; Shamim, Maha, and Imad Mazhal; Steve Allison; Janet Rachidi; Michael Birchell; Sam Fatima; Richard Monterosso; Lori Brandin; Elaine and Art Plumb; Phil Quirke; Tracey Springer; Howard and Marcia Trombley; Michelle Murphy; Suzanne Harrison; David Robin; Christine and Jill LaBeau; Ed Carlstedt; Rick D'Ascanio; Jeff Wallace; Tom Cook; Darren Broder; Sarah Sullivan; Angela Nicum; Sissy, Norman, Emily, and Kelly Breault; and to the students who inspired me to write this book: Ben Brickle, Misty Corio, Jon Lunt, Tanya Weeks, Chris White, Cassidy Tatro, Lynda Tenario, Cristina Supple, Amanda Defer, Josh Dellert, Frank Rodriguez, Tim Bartley, and Andy Bonin; and to all the students who studied under me during my tenure at Taconic High School, because you meant the world to me. I would like to further dedicate the book to the wonderful teachers at Lanesborough Elementary School and the education departments at MCLA and the University of Massachusetts at Amherst.

Thanks to my colleagues over the years in the British Council; the ministries of education in Tunisia, Algeria, UAE, Bahrain, Kuwait, Qatar, Russia, Ukraine, and Kyrgyzstan; Joe Paris of INS and his staff at the U.S. Embassy in Dushnanbe, Tajikistan; and, of course, the RELO officers, public affairs officers, and staff from the U.S. Department of State: Julia Walters, Agnes Ashton, Lisa Harshbarger, David Fay, John Scacco, Sami Saieed, Fatema Hashem, May Kakthuda, Margaret Combs and her staff at the American University in Kuwait, Guljan Tobleava, Alonya Sukininova, and Kathy Van De Vate. I also would like to thank state senator Ben Downing's office, representative Chris Speranzo's office, congressman Thomas Cole and the National Republican Small Business Advisory Board, the Massachusetts AMP coordinators, and SOMWBA. My deepest gratitude goes to all the teachers' unions, MATSOL, TESOL, TESOL Arabia, and Massachusetts Teachers Association, with a special dedication to Miles Stern, MCCC coordinators Joe Rizzo and Ellen Shanahan, Dawn Quinlin, and, of course, the best education lawyers I have proudly known to date: Michael Hinkley, Phillip Grandchamp, and Stephen Pagnotta, from Donovan and O'Connor, in North Adams, Massachusetts.

Introduction

This book will enlighten you about phrases used in the field of education. As a starting point, this introductory chapter will establish a basis for understanding how phrases or wordings may change according to context. Included in this book are phrases that should become standardized in the teaching profession.

Different Interpretations

It is always important to think about what you are saying and how it could be interpreted. Words can be misunderstood. Also, the meaning of words can be affected by the tone of the speaker's voice. For example, imagine if I said the following:

> *I* didn't steal your pink car. (Implies I was not involved with the theft)

When that sentence is repeated by others, a person might change the emphasis on any word, thus changing the entire meaning. Here is what that simple sentence could have turned into:

> I didn't *steal* your pink car. (Implies I borrowed it.)

> I didn't steal *your* pink car. (Implies I stole someone else's pink car.)

> I didn't steal your *pink* car. (Implies I stole your other-colored car.)

> I didn't steal your pink *car*. (Implies I stole your pink shirt, pink hat, or pink bicycle.)

This example allows you to see how the same sentence can take on very different meanings with different audiences because of the way it was understood. Sometimes we say things that we don't mean, but even when we say what we do mean, it can still be misunderstood by the listener.

Troublesome Words

Sometimes our words need clarification, so instead of explaining yourself, why not simply try to avoid certain words when possible? Three sample troublesome words are *always*, *never*, and *all*. I have found that at times, such as with rubrics, these terms are useful. However, when used to make broad statements, they leave the district and the teacher open for a possible attack by an angry parent or student:

> The dance has been canceled because a few people decided to . . .

The central problem here is that everyone suffers for the actions of a few. This approach might lead to frustration, retaliation, threats of a lawsuit, or a wide variety of other actions. Instead of the statement's dealing with specific individuals, everyone is grouped as part of the guilty party. The typical responses from parents and students might sound something like this:

> Well, why is everyone being punished? That is unfair.

> Why are all of them in trouble? My kid didn't do anything wrong. So, why should she be denied the opportunity to participate?

> Those teachers/administrators have some nerve. They are stopping my kid from participating. Why don't they deal with [name]? I know for a fact he/she is . . .

Now something simple has become complex. Such wording can cause a minor incident to snowball out of control. Let's look at another example. We've probably all caught ourselves saying to a parent,

"Johnny is never paying attention in my class. He is always talking with his friends."

What steps can we take to avoid such "danger words" as *always* and *never*? Your first step should be to think carefully about the statement. Let's revisit it: "Johnny is never paying attention in my class. He is always talking with his friends."

Upon hearing these words, the parent of a failing child, frustrated by the district, might seek legal action. Why? Because as the teacher, you have given the parent and the lawyer ammunition by saying that the child "never" pays attention. You have indirectly suggested that there is literally not one time that he listened to you in class. People might consider that premise ridiculous.

Take it a step further: what if the parent and lawyer can show that the student did for one moment listen to you? They have now discredited your words.

Let's take it even one step further than that: if you couple it with the second part of the statement, which suggests he is always talking with his friends, you better have documented all the friends he allegedly "always" talked to in your class. A clever lawyer would argue that your period is forty-five minutes long and that the child cannot speak continuously for forty-five minutes. Therefore, you could be portrayed as a teacher who exaggerates or worse.

If you are prone to using controversially interpreted words in the classroom, I have some suggestions and remedies to help you rephrase your comments. Here are some recommendations:

Instead of: He never listens.

Rephrase it: On the following documented days [list dates], it was noted that he was not listening. The topics discussed were _____ ; please note the correlation to his test scores on these topics.

Instead of: He is always talking.

Rephrase it: He was disrupting the class on the following dates [list dates] by talking during the class to friends. [Do not reveal the name of the students involved.]

Stating Opinions

In education, using words that convey your opinion is sometimes necessary in order to achieve your purpose. However, more often than not, these words can suggest that the speaker isn't flexible.

If a parent comes to the school to meet with you, it is nice to open a dialogue for communicative purposes. I think it is better to listen than to speak. Let's look at the next example:

> **Teacher:** I maintain my stance: he is lazy and not working up to his potential.
> **Parent:** My son is working hard.
> **Special education department (SPED) teacher:** He suffers from _____ , so he has difficulty focusing.
> **Teacher:** No. I am sorry, but there is no effort on his part.

In this situation, the teacher has stated an opinion without basis. The comments indicate that the teacher hasn't read the SPED or IEP document put in place by the school. The teacher has formed an opinion with little room for change. This situation is upsetting to the parent, who, in turn, can call the state's department of education and file a complaint against the school and/or teacher because the teacher is not in compliance with the educational plan required under federal law. Even the special education teacher is trying to hint to the colleague that there may be a physical or mental reason for the pupil's behavior, which might be beyond the child's control.

Using Demonstratives

Demonstratives—the infamous *this*, *that*, *these*, and *those*—can be sketchy to use. They are known to me as the devilish demonstratives.

They sound harmless, you say? Don't be fooled. Linguists will often tell you that these little words can cause problems because of their ambiguity. For one thing, they can serve as either pronouns or determiners in English. Moreover, the tricky little words create a sense of emotional distance, or even disdain, because of the meanings that can be derived from their usage. Don't believe me yet? Take a moment and think—what if you were to say the following as a teacher to a student:

This is the best you can do?

That is what you call homework?

These papers—well, what can I say?

Those opening sentences are supposed to alert the reader . . .

Imagine how these statements could be misused, taken out of context, misunderstood, or misinterpreted. A teacher who may be excellent in the classroom could be called into question for the way in which particular wording suggests negativity toward the student.

Instead of using demonstratives in your language, it frequently is better to be specific. For example, instead of talking about a student's paper as a whole, you should individualize the points, using constructive feedback. Let's look at the following phrases:

Instead of: This is the best you can do? That is what you are turning in to me for a grade?

Rephrase it (for a secondary/middle school student):
Although your paper isn't your best work to date, I liked
_____ , but we will need to reexamine _____ .
You'll need to show me how you arrived at your answers and how you intend to correct your work. I will expect the new submission by [date].

or

Rephrase it (for an elementary or early childhood student): This is a great letter *C*, but could you try to hold your pencil better to make it straighter? Come on, let's try by tracing my letter *C* together . . .

The goal is to get your students, parents, or administrators to understand what you want or need them to do. That is why after you relay the information, it is important to use a phrase that puts the responsibility for learning back on the student. For example:

Could you do this for me?

Show me that again.

Phrases to Absolutely Avoid

Oh, but the art of phrasing information doesn't stop there. Let's look at some more phrasing examples that could hurt your reputation, your teaching career, and the child entrusted into your care. Many are based on true-life experiences. I have heard teachers make these remarks to students. It is no wonder many students do not like going to school. It is bad enough that students are sometimes cruel to each other; they don't need teacher input to compound the distress. Here are some topics, words, and phrases that teachers should make a concerted effort to avoid:

- Any form of profanity or vulgarity in front of a child, including euphemisms such as "SOB."
- Referring to a child in slang terms, such as "cracker," "hippie," "dummy," "pothead," or "loser."
- Comments based on religion, such as "What are you, Jewish?" or "Are your parents Jesus freaks?"
- Referring to a specific group of children as "you people" or "your people."
- Plays on words that can be interpreted as racist, sexist, or hurtful. I once went to school with an African-American student named Barry. The teacher would say, "Do you know the answer, Blackberry?" Then she would joke, "I am just calling him a fruit." It wasn't nice, and almost thirty-five years later it still bothers me, because Barry dropped out of our private school.

- Remarks about a student's body shape or weight, such as "Eat something—you look anorexic," or the opposite: "What are you doing? It looks as if you are trying to grow man boobs!"
- Making sounds or hand gestures to imitate people with mental or physical handicaps.
- Pointing out a child's economic or class status, such as by saying, "What are you, Kenny from 'South Park'?"
- Any sexual connotation toward a student. A female teacher I worked with said to a girl in her senior class, "Well, I bet my man is better in bed than yours." The student complained to me (I was the department head), and I had to speak to the teacher, who didn't think she had said anything wrong!
- Discussing your weekend, family, or private life with students. You may think they are your friends, but they aren't. They are your pupils. Let them know only the essentials and only the positive things in your life.
- Hitting or touching a student. This includes pinching, swift kicks, whacks, and pats on any part of the body. Do not put students in a headlock, grab them, or shake them. Exceptions can be made for teachers licensed in restraints.
- Commenting on students' family or home life to them or to others. This includes making comments such as "Why does your mother put all her boyfriends before your welfare?" This type of situation is something to be discussed with the Department of Social Services (DSS) or a guidance counselor, not by you and the student. Although you care, you are not trained or licensed to be a psychologist or counselor.
- Commenting about a student's sexual preference or discriminating based on gender or other factors.
- Imposing your values. I have heard teachers do this in simple ways, such as by saying all of the following: "I don't believe in that kind of dancing; I think your dancing made you look like . . ." "Is your mother on crack? She lets you . . . ? No child of mine would be allowed to do that." "My dear, if I were your parent, you wouldn't be allowed to . . ." "Clearly, you are

7

raised in a godless home; I will pray for you." "Girls shouldn't be having babies out of wedlock."

The bottom line is to use common sense, and if you don't have a lot of common sense, attempt to find a mentor to help you make decisions. Under regular conditions, teachers should not inject their value systems or be judgmental.

Word Choices

It is in your best interest to think through your word choices. In this regard, a word to avoid is *claim*. In academic publications, it means one thing, but in an educational atmosphere, it often has a different connotation. For example, when a person uses *claims* in a construction such as "She claims to have . . ." it usually implies that the subject has acted or may act in a dishonest fashion. Now let's apply it in an educational setting.

A parent has come to see you. As the teacher, you say, "Well, your son claims . . . " This statement can cause animosity. Why? Instead of opening a line of communication, it has had the opposite effect. That simple phrase can imply that the person in question is up to something. It may sound as if you are mocking the son's words.

Here are some alternative suggestions that you could use that would be less offensive:

Your son alleges . . .

There are always two sides to a story. Your son's side of the story is . . . . The other student's side of the story is . . . . We are here today to find out what exactly happened and the order in which the events occurred.

Using Adjectives and Verbs

Wording and phrasing doesn't stop there. As a person in the field of education, you must be careful of how you use verbs and adjectives.

The use of the wrong verb or adjective can set you up for future problems. Let's say that I am overheard making a statement that uses the adjective *mad*, such as "Christine is mad." This can be interpreted as "Christine is crazy," or it can be interpreted as "Christine is angry."

As pointed out, some verbs can also make you sound defensive. For example, here are five words that are known to do this:

Insist
Maintain
Protest
Contend
Feel

These verbs should be used when you have proof, or when you are documenting an incident, such as in the following examples:

The district maintains, based on the documentation (see attached), that our exchange Gaelic teacher, Denise Withers, was correct when she contended . . .

According to Public Law No 94-142, established by Congress in 1975, it was found that there were more than eight million children with disabilities in the country and that more than half of them were not receiving an adequate education. We feel, after reviewing the compliance regulations, that the parent has the right to protest the appeal and decision of . . .

In oral conversations, on the other hand, verbs and adjectives such as these should be avoided when possible. When repeated by others, spoken words, unless they're taped, can change. So, I would avoid using these words in contexts such as the following:

Well, as the teacher of the class, I feel . . .

I maintain _____ , and nothing will change my mind.

I protest this student's chance of getting into an honors class. He isn't honors material.

9

As a veteran in education, I am cautious when I use certain words or phrases. Two other words that I hesitate to use are *just* and *only*. To be fair, these words are used quite often in education, because they usually suggest an unusual trait or ability that is measurable, such as in the following examples:

He is the only child in the second grade who is able to solve polynomials.

He just skipped three grades with his test scores.

But let's look at the problems that the words *just* and *only* can cause you when you use them in a different type of context:

Your child completes just the bare minimum to pass in my class.

He is passing only by the skin of his teeth.

Although each of these statements may be true, parents don't always take kindly to the truth. An angry parent would find instances in which the child completed more than "just the bare minimum" and would further argue that "passing only by the skin of his teeth" is truly an understatement, if not an unfair assessment. The reality is black and white: either the student passes or the student fails. Consequently, there is no need to qualify it with a remark that negates the facts. Thus, the grade, as a numerical average, should be able to stand on its own without commentary.

Chapter 1

Perfect Phrases for Communicating with the Parents of Your Students

As a teacher, you will involve yourself in many types of dialogues with a variety of people. In any reciprocal exchange between two or more parties, it is important to think before speaking. Communication is an art form, as it is the imparting or interchange of thoughts, opinions, or information by speech, writing, or signs to other people.

Two primary factors known to affect communication are auditory means and physical means. Auditory means, such as speaking, noises, and sometimes tone of voice, and nonverbal, physical means, such as body language, sign language, paralinguistic cues, eye contact, and touch, all have bearing on how the spoken message is interpreted by the listener. For example, the famed "teacher look," the glaring stare that can silence a class, may affect how students interpret expressions from other people they encounter in their life.

In a famed study by Mehrabian and Ferris (1967), it was estimated that 55 percent of impact is determined by body language (posture,

11

gestures, and eye contact), 38 percent by tone of voice, and only 7 percent by the content or words. If collaboration and cooperation are to occur between you as the teacher and the community, students, parents, and administrators, then processing, listening, observing, speaking, questioning, analyzing, and evaluating what is being said and what is heard is essential. This section of the book is intended to help you with phrasing greetings under a variety of circumstances, so that open lines of communication can exist in many forms.

Considerations When Greeting Parents

It is customary in Western culture to greet people with a firm handshake and to look them in the eye. However, as our populations become more diverse, so do our school districts. Be mindful of cultural sensitivities when greeting parents in more diverse school populations. Making the initial connection is essential to building a sound teacher-parent relationship.

When friction occurs between parents and teachers, the cause is often miscommunication. Teachers have been taught under a range of course styles, and their approaches may differ depending on their generation or on the region of the country. In addition, some have worked for other districts, whose policies may not be the same as those where they are currently teaching. For example, what may be acceptable with parents who are second- or third-generation Americans isn't always acceptable with those who are first-generation or are recent immigrants.

Moreover, some parents, because of their negative experiences in school, are constantly on the defensive. Other parents think they are the experts in how to teach materials. Some parents see you as a babysitter for six hours a day, while others expect you to make their child the next president of a major corporation. Each parent will be unique and will view the school from a unique perspective. This is why I try to ask parents the following questions when I meet them:

What was your experience like in school?

Which teacher were you most fond of, and which teacher did you despise?

What concerns do you have as a parent about your child's education?

The answers will vary from family to family. Knowing those answers will certainly help you understand your students and their families much better, making the educational experience more rewarding for everyone. Here are some additional phrases that may help you in satisfying the needs of a wide range of parents:

Do you have any questions before we begin?

Do you need bilingual services?

Do you need me to request a translator?

Have you been given a copy of our manual for parents?

Is there anything we can do to help you transition?

Is this your first time in an American school system?

What can the school do to accommodate your needs?

What special accommodations are necessary for our meeting?

Are you aware that the city/district/state offers you support services such as _____ free of charge or at a nominal fee?

Perfect Phrases for Parental Introductions

When greeting anyone, such as a parent, community member, or colleague, try to be polite. The Golden Rule generally applies. Your goal

13

is to look and to act like the professional that you are. In an academic environment, it is appropriate to start with a polite greeting. Here are some phrases you can use in an introductory greeting:

Good afternoon./Good evening./Good morning.

Good to see you. Won't you please sit down.

Hello, I am [your name]. I teach [grade or subject area] here at our school.

Do come in.

Hello. How are you?

How do you do? I am [your name], and you must be [parent's name].

I'm delighted to meet you. I'm glad you made the time to come in to see us.

I'm pleased to meet you.

Welcome. Please come inside and make yourself comfortable. Someone will be with you soon.

Perfect Phrases to Politely Excuse Yourself from a Conversation

When you need to excuse yourself from a conversation, don't just hope for a fire drill. There are ways to politely escape from the parent, administrator, or colleague who has engaged you in small talk. Here is a list of suggestions:

Do excuse me. I must go to my next class.

Good-bye. Again, thank you for making the time to come in and talk with us.

Good-bye. It was great talking with you.

I am sorry, but I have a class to prepare for.

I enjoyed having you here, but I am afraid I must go.

I enjoyed our conversation; we must do this again sometime.

I enjoyed talking to you, but I am afraid I'll have to cut our conversation short, because . . .

I enjoyed your visit. I wish I could stay longer to talk with you, but . . .

I had better be leaving or I will be late for . . .

I have a lot to do. Do excuse me.

I have a meeting that I have to prepare for.

I have a visitor coming, so I must prepare.

I have to get back to my next class.

I have to get going—the bell is about to ring.

I'm afraid I have to leave now, but it has been a pleasure.

I'm afraid it's time for me to go now.

I'm sorry you have to go, but to be truthful, so do I.

I'm very happy to meet you. I wish we could have talked longer, but I have to . . .

It has been a pleasure. If you are free at a later time, I'd like to talk more with you.

It has been interesting to speak with you. I feel bad because I have to run.

It is good to see that you are open to further discussion. Won't you please come to my office/classroom on another day that is more convenient for both of us so we can talk further ?

Oh, look at the time; I have an appointment that I am going to be late for if I don't hurry.

I have to get back to class.

Well, I see it's getting late. I'd better go.

Well, I should be going now. I do hope you understand.

Perfect Phrases for Closing a Conversation with a Parent

The end of the meeting needs to be like the opening: polite, considerate, and professional. This is why it is advantageous to have shorter and more general conclusive phrases to end the conversation. Here are some closing phrases that can prove useful:

I hope to see you again in the near future.

If I don't see you again, have a nice weekend.

I'll see you later. When will you be back?

I'll talk to you later.

It was nice talking to you.

It was really good talking to you.

It's been a pleasure to meet you.

It was nice to meet you.

Nice to meet you [shake hands].

See you later.

See you soon, I hope.

Take care of yourself.

Talk to you later.

Thank you for making the time to meet with us today.

Thank you for stopping in.

Thanks for coming.

We hope to see you at our school and its events again.

Perfect Phrases for Greeting Parents Who Corner You

If you are a teacher, you have learned that many parents value their time, but not yours. They think you are on the clock whenever they run into you. If you are new to teaching, you will learn quickly that as an educator, you are accosted by parents, "concerned" citizens, and others at sporting events, while shopping, at home, or at social gatherings. The phrases that follow can help you politely extricate yourself from the conversation:

I have people with me. So, I can't really talk right now.

I wish I could stay and talk with you, but it would make me late for my next appointment.

It would be inappropriate for me to comment here in public. Come by my classroom next week so we can talk.

This isn't a good time right now. Could we schedule an appointment during school hours next week?

This probably isn't the best place to talk. Call me next week, and we'll chat after school.

You will have to forgive me, but I don't have the appropriate time it will take to discuss this and offer it the attention it deserves.

Perfect Phrases to End Uncomfortable Conversations

If you find yourself involved in a situation in which the topic turns to something you don't wish to discuss, you can end up between a rock and a hard place. On one hand, it is paramount that you be polite to the members of your school community. On the other hand, you are not obligated to participate in conversations that make you uncomfortable. The following phrases are useful when you want to move a conversation along without really commenting on anything. They will allow you to remain polite and professional:

From the onset, I have to be honest: I am unable to comment or offer assistance to you. I can recommend people you could talk to.

I am not trying to give the appearance that I am not interested or that I don't care, because I do care. You have to understand: I am unable to speak to the topic at this time.

I am unable to do anything about it at this time. I have so many things on my plate. Could you write it down for me? Send it to me by letter or e-mail, and I will respond accordingly.

I don't feel it is appropriate for me to comment or to be a part of this conversation. You will have to excuse me.

I hope you understand that I cannot comment on the progress of other students. The student's academic progress and information is protected under the Federal Educational Rights and Privacy Act (FERPA).

I understand your concern, but I have no knowledge or authority regarding this matter. If you would like to contact our principal, I am sure he/she would set up a meeting with you.

I want to talk to you about this in depth. However, this isn't the appropriate setting to do so. Why don't you get in touch with me sometime next week? And thank you for understanding my position.

If you don't mind, I would like to avoid this conversation with you. If you insist on speaking to me about this, I ask that we set up a formal meeting with specialists from the school. I hope you will cooperate with this request.

Oh boy, I don't know anything about this, but you know who might: [cite name]. I hope this helps.

This is not a good time for me. I would love to talk with you, but we need to schedule a future time or date. Is that possible?

This isn't the appropriate meeting place to discuss this.

This isn't the time or place for this conversation. Why don't you stop in during the school day and make an appointment to see me about this?

We've known each other for a long time, and I wish I could be of further assistance, but honestly, I don't have any input on this matter. You know, maybe, you would want to contact _____ instead? It is just a suggestion.

You know, I would be glad to talk to you about this in private. Would you mind stepping outside—or, better yet, my free period is from _____ to _____ ; could you meet with me then?

Perfect Phrases to Diffuse Gossip and Unwanted Comments

If a parent or colleague is overheard making unwanted comments or adding fuel to gossip, your first reaction may be to confront the speaker to put a stop to the situation. For example, a teacher notes to her colleagues that she saw a fax in the main office suggesting a student be given a waiver to graduate without going to summer school. She assumes that the principal changed the grade, although there was nothing in the fax to indicate that that was the case. Another teacher overhears this conversation and knows the student to whom the speaker was referring; she repeats what she has learned to another colleague, the faculty member who assigned the failing grade. That faculty member first confronts the student and then storms into the main office with unfounded accusations. Chaos reigns based on unfounded gossip. It is often better to enlist the aid of a neutral third party and call a meeting. The important thing is that you nab the issue as soon as possible before the gossip grows and can't be stopped. You have to remain the professional, because your job and reputation depend on it. Don't blow up! Just walk in to the meeting as if nothing has happened, and be sure to use a neutral tone. Here are some examples of what you might say:

Is it true that you said _____ to _____ in reference to me?

It has come to my attention that you may have been speaking about me negatively in public. Your words could be misconstrued as slander.

There are some allegations that you may have said _____ and attached my name to it.

Could you explain to me how your name got attached to this story that is being spread about me?

I understand you have concerns about my teaching ability. I welcome you to make an appointment to see me teach a class. To date, you haven't been in my classroom, but it is my understanding that you are publicly commenting about my professionalism and ability to command a classroom. This is very disturbing to me.

Would you be willing to clear up some allegations about some comments you may have made in regard to me?

We are here today because I have some growing concerns that involve your allegedly misusing my name. I would like to clear up some rumors that have come back to me.

Thank you for meeting with me.

Good to see you again. What is it that you would like to discuss, because I understand you have some concerns about me as a teacher?

Please don't misquote me in public.

Please don't take what I have said out of context.

This is my personal point of view and doesn't necessarily reflect the district's views.

What was said was not for public consumption. I thought you would have had the integrity to respect that.

What I am saying is off the record . . . [But remember: it is always on the record.]

I don't wished to be quoted, so I am willing to speak with you off the record. Are you agreeable to this condition?

Perfect Phrases for When You Are Unexpectedly Called to a Meeting

Sometimes you are pulled into a meeting with an agenda that hasn't been fully described to you or for which you did not have adequate time to prepare. In such circumstances, the most important thing is not to get flustered. Put the burden on the back of the person who called the meeting. To get through such an unexpected situation while maintaining appearances, you may want to use these phrases:

Could you let me know what the primary objective is of your meeting with me today?

It is my understanding that you wish to discuss an issue with me today. Could you elaborate?

[As the other party talks, nod and smile, complemented by facial expressions that indicate that you are listening, though you may be totally in the dark.] Oh, really? Hmm. Interesting.

[End the conversation on a neutral note.] It was good hearing from you. I will take it under consideration.

Be sure to follow along and to respond appropriately. Here are other possible ways to end the meeting:

Thank you for coming in to speak with me today about your concerns.

I assure you that what you have heard is untrue. I do appreciate your coming in and speaking to the concern. Not many parents care enough to do this. Again, thank you for coming in today.

This has been a very interesting conversation. I am glad we were able to clear the air and dispel such vicious rumors. Thank you for your concern and time. We hope this matter is now cleared up.

Perfect Phrases for Unannounced Parental Visits

If you are surprised by a visit from a parent, you essentially have two options. First, you can step outside and ask the visitor to wait a moment until you are finished. Even if you are free, take the moment and get any needed copies, materials, or grade books in order before sitting down with the parent. Second, if the timing is not convenient, thank the parent for stopping in, pull out a date book, and schedule a meeting for a date that works for both of you.

For several reasons, it is not a good idea to allow a parent or guardian to come into your classroom while you are teaching. If someone should try to just walk in and sit down, you must contact the office, as the person's presence may be in violation of Criminal Offender Record Information (CORI) law. This person may not be the custodial guardian or parent and may pose an uncomfortable presence to the child involved. Also, other students' confidential information could be breached. In a worst-case scenario, the person may have a weapon or may have ingested a substance prohibited in schools.

If someone insists on meeting with you immediately, and you are not free, send the person to guidance or the office. The staff there will decide whether classroom coverage is needed for you to attend an immediate meeting with the appropriate parties and whether you must be pulled from your lesson to discuss the parent's concern. Here are phrases you can use in this type of situation:

> *You need to meet me during my free period. I am teaching my class right now.*

> *Have you signed in at the office? I can't meet with you; I am in the middle of teaching my class.*

> *I can't speak to you right now. By law, I must directly supervise my students.*

> *I realize this is the lunch period, but I am on cafeteria duty today. I must supervise the students.*

Perfect Phrases for Correspondence

It is often necessary to contact parents by phone, letter, or e-mail. There are certain safeguards to employ in this regard:

- Clear your communication with the administration.
- Keep a general phone log with dates and topics.
- Be careful what message you leave on an answering machine, because of privacy laws.
- Speak only to the direct guardian about the purpose of the call.

By Phone

Many parents are working and not available when a teacher calls. Most times, you will have to speak to an answering machine. Here is a sample message that has proven effective:

Hello. This is [your name] from [name of school]. I am calling to speak to [name of parent or guardian]. I would like to invite you to meet with me and others to discuss [child's name]'s progress. I am hoping you are free to meet on [day], which is the [date], at around [time]. If this is not convenient for you, please let us know, and we will reschedule. Otherwise, we will expect to see you then to discuss [child's name]. If you have any questions, call me at [phone number].

By E-Mail

If you decide to send the invite by e-mail, then you might want to use the following:

Dear [name]:

Let me introduce myself. I am [your name] from [name of school]. I teach your child's [subject] class. I would like to schedule a meeting with you to discuss [child's name]'s progress in my course. If you could select one of the following dates and times to meet with me, it would be appreciated. If none of the choices is convenient, please contact me to make alternate arrangements.

Yours in good faith,

[your name, department, name of school, and contact information]

By Formal Letter

If the parent or guardian does not have a telephone or Internet access, you may want to post a letter. If so, use your school letterhead, and send a copy of the correspondence to the guidance counselor for the student's file. Here is an example:

[school letterhead]
[recipient address]
[date]

Dear Mr. and Mrs. [name]:

My name is Mrs. [name]. I am your child's seventh grade creative writing teacher. Ms. [name], your child's guidance counselor, and I would like to schedule a thirty-minute meeting on [date] to discuss [child's name]'s progress. Please let us know what time would be most convenient for you to meet.
To set up a time, or if you have questions, please contact [contact name and phone number].

Sincerely,

[your name, course, department]

Home Visitation

If you need to go to the home because the parent does not respond to your telephone call, e-mail, or letter, you should always enlist a colleague or other witness to accompany you. You should also inform the guidance office and/or principal's office of your intent to visit a student's home. This step is for your protection, as your visit may be interpreted differently at a later date.

Before going to a home, find out the district's policy for such visits. Next, ask superiors what should and should not be said to the parent, and ask for information regarding any previous contacts and relationships between the district and the party. Do not take it upon yourself to act without prior approval. In many instances, a home visit crosses a line that needs to be supported by the teacher's administration.

One final note on this subject: It is advisable to never give a student a ride home. It is prudent to conduct all business with students in the actual school building during hours when other people are present with an open door unless other witnesses are present.

Chapter 2

Perfect Phrases for Parent-Teacher Conferences

Parent-teacher conferences should occur at minimum once a year. These brief meetings between students' parents and teachers should be treated like interviews. The interview is a chance for parents to get to know their child's teachers and review any issues or concerns that the parents or teachers may have with the student's behavior or academic performance.

These interviews are usually five to fifteen minutes in length, so it's necessary to condense the bigger picture into an "elevator speech" about the child and the issues the child is facing. Each interview will be different, because each child has a specific set of needs. Regardless of the circumstances of a given case, you cannot ignore the areas that need improvement.

The dynamics of the parental encounter vary widely. Some parents will want to dictate to you how you should be teaching, despite the fact that they aren't licensed and haven't completed a professional teacher-training program. Some parents will be angry or upset or may even come across as not wanting or liking their own children. Others will be indifferent—and, of course, some will be super parents.

During parent-teacher conferences, I have seen the gamut of responses, but no matter what happens, you have to remember that you are the observer trained to report on how the child is progressing in the school environment. This chapter is going to teach you how to cope with a variety of scenarios, as well as encourage you to schedule follow-up meetings with parents, accompanied by counselors, to further discuss the needs of the child when necessary.

Some schools have implemented electronic interviews, which can be a more complicated issue, as the information is transmitted in written form. Keep in mind that what you say orally dissipates in the air, while what you put in writing can survive for centuries. The teacher is safer having written documentation as long as it is written in a neutral tone and shows objectivity. This is why you should pay careful attention to how you word information given to a parent in the interview or conference process.

Perfect Phrases for Welcoming Parents into the Classroom

If you invite parents to a conference (or to meet with you at any other time), it is important to welcome them and to thank them for taking the time to come in to see you. Here are some phrases that can help you do that:

You must be [parent's name]. It is a pleasure to finally meet you.

Please come on in. I have been expecting you.

Hello, I am [your name]. And you must be [child's name]'s parents/guardians.

I am so glad you could make this meeting.

So, you must be [child's name]'s parent. I am happy to finally be meeting you.

Won't you please come in and take a seat.

Where would you like to sit?

What would make you feel most comfortable?

Can I get you something before we begin?

I have set up an area over there where we can speak.

Perfect Phrases for Opening a Parent Conference

For all parties to get the most out of a parent-teacher conference, it is beneficial for you to have phrases ready to start a profitable discussion about the student. Here are some positive phrases to use to express individual comments about a child:

I love teaching your child!

School is proving difficult for your child, but I have seen [child's name] make great improvements in the past weeks.

Your child goes beyond expectations. This is best demonstrated by . . .

Your child has a great sense of humor.

Your child has been a wonderful helper.

Your child has been strong in [identify areas of achievement] and not so strong in [identify areas needing improvement].

Weaknesses are noted in these areas . . .

The child is most challenged in the areas of [list] . . .

Your child has expressed interest in . . .

Your child has to learn how to . . .

Your child can memorize chunks of information.

Your child is a good candidate for . . .

Your child is a logical thinker.

Your child is a love to have in class.

Your child is a special individual, and it has been a privilege to teach him/her.

Your child is polite, smart, and a joy to teach.

Your child is kind to others.

Your child is self-motivated.

Your child is showing leadership potential.

Perfect Phrases for Reinforcing Positive Behavior

For every challenge that you will encounter with a particular student, you will also see many positive areas or areas in which the child has improved. If you are going to cite a negative, try to find two positives to counteract your statement. For example, here are some positive statements that show that the student has potential as a learner:

Your child wrote this paper [show the parent the paper hanging on the wall].

Your child understands how to . . .

Your child welcomes new information.

Your child's competencies are best demonstrated in this piece of work . . .

Your child's potential is endless.

Your child's project was exceptional.

Your child's strengths can best be demonstrated by . . .

Your child's work is complete and concise and shows effort.

Look at this work that [child's name] gave me just last week.

Sometimes [child's name] will tell me he can't do something, when in fact—look at this [show the parent the completed assignment]—he can. This is a good piece of work. Look how he . . .

Your child has a thorough understanding of the steps involved in . . .

Look how your child was able to extract applicable information.

He/she has met or exceeded expectations in the areas of . . .

One of the strengths that I have noticed is . . .

I like watching how he/she strategically partners up with [classmate's name].

[child's name] has a keen eye for detail.

Your child can express himself/herself through the arts. Look at this. . . . He/she doesn't hesitate to ask a question if something is unclear. That is a good sign.

Your child is able to identify more efficient ways of getting through the material.

I think your child is working to develop critical thinking skills. He/she can think outside the box.

Let me be the first to tell you, I am very impressed with [child's name]'s ability to . . .

Perfect Phrases for Opening Conversations Regarding Concerns

It can be difficult to hear negative things about one's child. I have seen parents cry in response. This is because parents are human, and most parents love their children. As a teacher, you have a duty to be honest, because you want to show areas where the learner can improve. Let's look at two approaches:

The inappropriate approach: *Yeah, none of the other kids like your son. I can't blame them. You know he is socially inept. It is like he is the gross kid.*

The appropriate approach: *Your child is having some challenges with social interactions with peers.*

Listed here is a series of productive approaches for describing concerns to parents and guardians. Each of these should serve as a template to be adapted to fit the particular case:

Your child has improved by leaps and bounds, but I still have some concerns. I've noticed . . .

Your child has been teased or feels threatened by . . .

You child is sensitive to . . .

Your child can think in the abstract but has difficulty with . . .

Your child concerns me because lately I have noticed . . .

Perfect Phrases for Helping Students Experiencing Difficulties

Sometimes you will need to make suggestions or recommendations to which parents aren't going to be open, because they will disagree with your assessment. In anticipation of such a reaction, it is wise to preface your statement with a softening comment. For example:

This is only a suggestion that might help [child's name].

I have a recommendation for you. Would you be open to hearing it?

Then you must describe what you want as the end result. Here are some perfect phrases to help you, in your most sincere voice, explain to parents what might be in the best interest of their child:

Your child may be better suited to . . .

Your child may be eligible for _____ ; would you be open to that?

Your child may need to be tested for . . .

Your child overreacts to certain situations, so I would like to get him/her in a program for . . .

Your child sees beyond the basics. I would like to challenge him/her by . . .

Your child should be considered for . . .

Your child took the initiative to _____ and might like being a part of . . .

Your child makes an effort to learn materials but is having difficulties. I would like to get him/her tested for . . .

Your child tries to influence others, and I think it is because he/she is hoping . . .

Your child would best be served if we . . .

Perfect Phrases for Describing Behaviors That Might Require Intervention

In some instances, you will need to discuss behaviors that might call for intervention from the school's psychologist, peer counselor, or nurse. Sometimes, when you say that you want the child to see the school's psychologist, the parent can go ballistic and will immediately protest, "My kid is not crazy."

Here are some phrases that you can use to diffuse these particular situations:

Your child is being ridiculed, and it is affecting his/her schoolwork.

Your child is a victim of rumors.

Your child is showing signs of depression.

Your child is acting out.

Your child is demonstrating abnormal behaviors.

Your child is experiencing anxiety.

Your child is having a difficult time with self-acceptance.

Your child is having trouble focusing.

Your child is influenced easily by peers.

Perfect Phrases for Describing Inappropriate Behaviors

In some instances, you have to dance lightly around the topic; but in other instances, you must be up-front with the parent. Make sure the parent knows that you are conveying this information in order to self-correct an issue that could hinder the child's learning. Here are some common behaviors that must be addressed and discussed:

Your child daydreams in class.

Your child is not meeting expectations.

Your child has major breakdowns.

Your child has minor meltdowns.

Your child has shown signs of . . .

Your child has shown tendencies of violence and has threatened others.

Your child has used inappropriate language in my classroom.

Your child is acting up.

Your child is not applying himself/herself.

Your child is aware of the rules and yet continues to . . .

Your child is bullying others.

Your child is constantly trying to leave class to visit the nurse or the bathroom or wander the halls.

Your child is failing to complete assignments.

Your child is falling behind.

Your child is finding the material too easy.

Your child is not living up to his/her potential.

Your child is struggling.

Your child is very curious about _____ but in a negative way.

Your child lacks an appropriate attention span.

Your child hates school.

Your child made this [show the project of concern].

Your child's work doesn't appear to be his/her own.

Perfect Phrases for Addressing Seriously Inappropriate Behaviors

Being direct with parents about student behaviors is imperative. Skirting issues and turning a blind eye to situations just causes the next teacher to have more problems. Here are some phrases that can help you to pinpoint problems:

[child's name] needs to demonstrate more restraint.

[child's name] ridicules classmates. We are meeting today to work toward changing this behavior.

[child's name] shows little self-control.

An impartial look at [child's name]'s behavior may further suggest . . .

As the parent, you have input that is instrumental to your child's success.

Bizarre responses by your child to standard questions have raised some flags of concern.

Clowning around in class is unacceptable behavior.

His/her boisterousness is causing many disruptions to the learning environment.

I am not seeing signs of temperance when it comes to issues of . . .

I have watched your child's inappropriate responses, which have included raising his/her fists.

I haven't seen signs of reasonableness.

On occasion, your child has a tendency to lose control.

Passively sitting by, saying nothing, is not going to change the situation.

Please do not be misled by . . .

Please don't tell yourself that this problem will go away.

Ridiculous behaviors such as the ones demonstrated must be addressed.

Slapstick antics have been very disruptive.

The deep intensity of your child's _____ concerns me.

The ferocity of intent to get what your child wants when he/she wants it concerns me.

The lack of stimulation provided to the child concerns me.

There is a chance that your child is predisposed to _____ ; this is why we are asking for a formalized test/program.

This is a give-and-take relationship; therefore, it is important that you . . .

Unfortunately, your child has been a subject of ridicule.

Viciously attacking your child's classmates is not productive and won't be tolerated.

We are trying to maintain neutrality, but your actions are making that more difficult.

We ask that you aid us in this endeavor.

We have noticed that when things don't go your child's way, he/she has a violent temper.

We need to find a happy medium in order to survive the year with each other.

Wisecracks have caused disruption to the learning environment.

You are showing signs of aggressive behavior.

You are misdirected if you think . . .

You are not promoting the learning environment that would be ideal to best help your child.

Your child shows signs of abnormal agitation when questioned or confronted.

Your child dashes around at the last minute trying to get assignments done. If we could work together, I would like to help your child change this bad habit by . . .

Your child has not completed . . .

The student has transferred from _____ and is currently lagging behind in this school.

The student has used nepotistic ties by suggesting that because you work in the school district, he or she is allowed to . . .

Your child is demonstrating a fiery personality, which isn't helping us get to a resolution.

Your child is having difficulty gauging fairness.

Your child's fuming over the issue isn't going to solve the problem.

Chapter 3

Perfect Phrases for Dealing with Problematic Parents

In educational situations, dealing with difficult parents is part of the job. Sometimes you will work with parents who may come across as problematic because of their attitude or personality. Do not mistake these parents with those who seek guidance from you. During your career, parents who are at a loss about what to do with their child will come to you for advice because you are trained to work with children and your profession is to help them become sound citizens. In these situations, you can share your views or refer parents to a federal government resource such as usa.gov/topics/parents_education.shtml, which offers information on topics ranging from preventing bullying, returning to school, and helping children with learning disabilities.

Problematic parents are most likely problematic people in other areas of their lives outside of school. They often expect patience and understanding from others but will not reciprocate. These types of parents tend to be conflicted people who may push you to your limits, but you must try to remain composed and professional despite their behavior. As a rule, dealing with a problematic parent is easier when the person is just generally obnoxious or when the behavior affects multiple people. Dealing with problematic parents is much tougher when they are attacking you directly or undermining your professional contribution or teaching efforts in the classroom.

That said, a parent who is difficult or problematic for a first-year teacher may have no effect on a veteran teacher ready for retirement. As a teacher, you must remember that the degree of difficulty you face in dealing with a person depends in large part on your self-esteem, your self-confidence, and your professional experience. Throughout your career, you may have to deal with the dysfunctional aspects of people's behaviors or actions, because that is who they are. This section will help you with phrasing good conversational responses.

Perfect Phrases to Describe Parents to Administrators

If a confrontation occurs between you and a parent, it is critical that you inform your administrator. For one thing, the administrator would like a "heads-up" before the parent barges into the office complaining! It may then turn out that you will be placed in charge of a meeting or course of action to address the situation, or you may need to follow up on the incident. You will have to accurately report the parental behavior—verbal as well as nonverbal—to administrators, which may then lead to face-to-face accountability.

While some parents will avoid confrontation for fear the teacher will retaliate in the classroom, other parents will not hesitate to address their issues with you. Depending on the nature of the confrontation, the following phrases can help you in your efforts to explain the parent to the administrator. This approach will allow the administrator to formulate a plan to ameliorate the situation as may be needed.

[child's name]'s parents have been cooperative.

The parents of students attending have been instrumental and actively involved in _____ .

[child's name]'s parents will be ejected from school events if they . . .

The parents have denied that their child has _____ despite . . .

*During a parent meeting, [parent's name] was acting
_____ ; the behavior included . . . . I felt that, as the
administrator, you should know.*

*I would like to take a minute to give you a heads-up that the
mother or father of [child's name] might stop in to see you.
They were not pleased with the information I had conveyed to
them about their son/daughter at the parent conference.*

*The other evening at the parent conference, [parent's
name] became explosive when it was suggested that her
son/daughter's performance was . . . . I followed policy and
procedure, showing her the grades, but instead was greeted
with insults and anger. You or a guidance counselor might be
needed to intervene, since her reaction was so extreme.*

*On [date], I met with [parent's name], whose child [child's
name] is in my [subject] class. Using a professional tone and
an objective manner, I showed her both the strengths and
weaknesses of the child's performances. She disagreed with
my judgment and stated . . . . Although nothing may come
of this confrontational situation, I wanted to document the
incident for the guidance counselor and administration,
should further problems arise.*

*I just wanted to ask if we could discuss a particular parental
conference that I found disturbing. I would like to get your
advice about how you, as my mentor and my administrator,
would like me to handle the situation if it were to occur again.*

Perfect Phrases for Dealing with the "Helicopter" Parent

The "helicopter" mom or dad is the parent who hovers over every
move the child makes. This moniker describes the mom who wants
to clean her child's locker, complain about her child's grade, and intervene with her child's friends. It also applies to the dad who fills out job

applications and may actually try to interview on behalf of his child. Helicopter parents circle around and suffocate the child because they think that they know best. Recognize these helicopter parents, and quietly clip their wings!

Most veteran teachers and administrators would advise you not to give in to these types of parents, because doing so will only lead to further trouble down the line. When an incident happens, notify the administration. To potentially curb it from happening a second time, use some of the following phrases:

Why isn't your child bringing this concern to me? Does he/she know that you are here?

This is an abnormal situation. I advise that we arrange a meeting with both your child and the guidance counselor present.

This meeting and your actions overstep the boundaries. I am going to suggest we . . .

It is evident that you love your child and are looking out for his/her best interests, but it is your child who needs to take the initiative to . . .

I understand your concerns, but I am going to continue to teach the curriculum.

School is a place where your child will grow and develop into the person your child wants to be. We cannot dictate how your child's life should be lived, but what we can do is facilitate the learning that takes place.

Would you be agreeable to an action plan and a follow-up meeting with me and perhaps a team of your child's teachers, with an administrator present, so that we can openly discuss your concerns and answer any questions you may have about the growth, development, and academic learning of your child?

I have noticed that you pay extremely close attention to your child's experiences and problems, particularly at our school, and I admire you for it. However, it seems to me that you may want to consider . . .

In your rush to prevent any harm or failure from befalling your child, you are denying your child the opportunity to learn from making mistakes. I know that it is a hard thing to do as a parent, but you need to try to slowly let go and allow [child's name] to make independent decisions.

You are trying too hard to smooth out and remove all obstacles for your child and, in doing so, are actually crippling the learning experiences. I want to sit down and just talk to you about some ideas that might help you help your son/daughter without doing it for your son/daughter.

Perfect Phrases for Dealing with the "Here They Come Again" Parent

Some parents seem to live vicariously through their children, almost as if they are getting a second chance to go to school. Although their intentions may very well be good, they always manage to stir things up. Sometimes you may feel that you can't get anything done when they're around. They're criticizing, they're correcting, and they're meddling. They're giving you all the reasons they think that you should do this or that.

These parents have the potential to become your biggest headache. Therefore, it is vital that you keep the situation under your own control by taking the following actions:

- Erect boundaries by creating before- or after-school office hours. If this tactic doesn't work, reschedule meetings and events for times that may not be convenient for them.
- Limit contact by appointments, and politely discourage drop-in visits.

- Limit the context of your meetings to school hours only, and cite the union contract as your excuse.
- Keep the overbearing parents and guardians on friendly terms, and don't let them catch on that you are controlling the situation using manipulative means.

Be aware: these people often don't get the hint. Or if they do get the hint, they assume it doesn't apply to them. Here are some phrases to help you back them off:

Which days did you say you couldn't come? [Let them answer.] Oh dear, I have to check something. I am almost sure that is when we were looking to plan _____; maybe it can be changed. I will check and get back to you. [Wait on getting back to them, but do follow through at some point.]

The role of volunteering is arranged through our PTA. I suggest you go through those channels.

Have you registered at the office to report that you are in the building? The procedure is part of the security program we are implementing.

I have a day once a week that I meet with parents. If you don't mind, I will make you an appointment.

The union/district policy does not allow me to _____; I do hope you understand.

Absolutely, I would love to have you on board. I have an idea for a project that you could do that is coming up. Leave me your details, and I will get back to you in a few weeks.

I am sorry, but parents aren't allowed to wander the halls or open student lockers without permission. I am going to have to ask you to leave.

This is a student-only area.

Is the office aware you are here? I don't see a badge.

Parents are welcome to participate in _____ , but I'm afraid they can't disrupt lessons for . . .

I am surprised to see you here again. Where do you find the time?

Perfect Phrases for Dealing with Overbearing Parents

Overbearing parents can be overwhelming with their need for dominance. These types of people can sometimes be wearing on the spirit and can become more aggressive over time if not dealt with in a professional but firm manner. They may appoint themselves as the classroom moms or dads, even when they don't need to be at the school. Here again, it is incumbent on you to erect boundaries.

When dealing with overbearing people, be choosy about what information you share. You're not obliged to reveal everything about your life to anyone. If your gut tells you that something is better left unsaid, then go with that thought.

You may find that overbearing parents will use a statement out of context against you to get what they want. An overbearing person can have a hold on different aspects of your life, causing you to harbor hostility and resentment. Because they affect you emotionally, you may be goaded to say something that you will later regret.

In light of these circumstances, an impartial outsider may be needed to move things forward and to intercede with these types of people. Often the overbearing person doesn't know when to stop or call it quits. Here are some phrases to help you in your interactions with overbearing people—parents as well as colleagues and others:

Clearly, you are a strong force, but I will have to agree at this time to differ with you.

I am afraid we will need to continue this meeting at another time.

45

I believe that the information you should have received was . . .

I feel that you are being antagonistic toward the situation. May I suggest you take a different approach.

I feel you are coming on a little strong.

I think it would be better if a third party were present and served as a witness to this discussion.

I think this conversation is inappropriate at this time.

I think you may have been misinformed.

I understand your desire to _____ , but to take it upon yourself to _____ is not the wisest decision at this time.

It appears that you are vehemently opposed to _____ , as we are unable to come to an understanding. Is it possible to suggest to me what you would like to see happen?

It is easy to suppose _____ , but to presume is not prudent at this time.

It is easy to understand your concern, but you need to back down a little and give us a moment to look at this situation rationally.

It is presumptuous to think . . .

It would help the situation if you would contain yourselves a bit more. Your actions and words could be misconstrued as arrogant.

If talking to an overbearing parent fails to bring improvement, depending on the situation, you may want to try to put the overbearing personality to constructive use. Sometimes parents who want to control or be a part of everything in the school just don't have enough going on in their own lives. If there's no getting rid of them, at least make their compulsions work for you: give them a task or project to complete.

First, consider putting them in charge if possible. Second, recognize their need to be recognized. Third, let them know what it is like to put in hours of work to accomplish something only to be criticized. Here are some phrases to lure them into "helping out" and eventually "getting out" of your hair:

What I need you to do . . .

Then, I expect you will want to run our . . .

I think you should get involved and lead our . . .

What if I left you in charge of _____; you could run our _____ , don't you agree?

If you show this kind of passion toward improving our school, I think you should be made . . . . I am definitely giving the principal and the PTA your name and contact information.

In the case of an overbearing parent who has no intention of helping out and will only continue offering unsolicited advice, my suggestion is that you listen. Yes, listen to what the person has to say—and then respond that you can't act upon the "advice" until the parent puts it in writing. People don't like putting things in writing and signing their names. I have eliminated 70 percent of my potential workload with that simple suggestion. Here are some phrases to help you lead up to that request:

I can't really act upon your suggestion until you send me a formal request in writing with your commitment to . . .

In order for me to go forth with this, it is important that you put it in writing and send it to me.

Thanks again for caring enough to bring _____ to our attention. Can you put that in writing?

I will share your concerns with _____ once I receive your comments in writing. Thanks for coming in today, and I look forward to reading your written requests.

Your input will be taken under consideration once your proposal has been received.

I am glad you shared your ideas. I will mention them to others on the team once you send them in writing to us.

Perfect Phrases for Confronting Improper Parents

Improper parental behavior is on the rise. Many parents seem to feel that they can be abusive to faculty and staff and be beyond reproach. There are documented cases of parents physically or verbally abusing teachers or of schools removing parents from the grounds due to improper behavior, especially at sporting events. Parents have written blogs that negatively affect the teacher's reputation. I remember a case in which a parent, furious because her child had been caught with alcohol, told the school that she provided the alcohol and allowed the child to drink it and that it wasn't the school's right to interfere in such a matter. If you have to engage with these types of guardians, you may achieve the best outcome by phrasing your remarks as follows:

Confrontational behavior is not going to help resolve this situation.

Is there a reason you are continuing to argue the point? I thought it was just resolved.

It is discourteous to _____ ; it would be more than fair to say . . .

No one is disputing the fact, so I can't understand why you are getting so upset.

One could think by your response that you are being . . .

Please be aware of your tone.

Please do not act bad-mannered in my presence.

Please stop. No one is fighting with you over this point. Instead, let's look at the situation from a logical standpoint, using reason instead of fists.

There is no need for this situation to come to blows.

There is no need to be argumentative.

There is no need to be boorish.

There is no need to wage war.

This approach is making our meeting very awkward.

This is a simple skirmish.

This is not a battle. It is a simple misunderstanding that resulted from miscommunication. I think we can resolve all parties' concerns by sitting down and listening to one another.

This is not a competition in which one child is better than another. You need to stop putting such intense pressure on [child's name].

We ask that you cease being disrespectful.

We ask that you control the volume of your voice.

We can't scrap the entire program, as you are suggesting, but we can modify it.

We have struggled with the situation, and we feel . . .

We have wrestled with the thought of . . . what do you think?

*We hope this meeting will be nonconfrontational. We ask all
parties to avoid being quarrelsome.*

What do you suggest would be a fair trade-off?

Perfect Phrases for Dealing with Angry Parents

Dealing with angry people is never easy. Sanity often gets thrown
out the window as people react instead of thinking. Anger can come
about when people believe that a wrong has been done to someone
or something close to them. Science has shown us that a mother bear
will protect her cubs at any cost. An enraged mother—or father—of
the human species also can be dangerous. For the benefit of everyone involved, you want to quell the anger and to calm the parent
down. Here are some phrases to keep in your arsenal:

*I can see that you are annoyed. What would you like me to do
to help your child?*

*I can feel your irritation. It is understandable. What can we do
to alleviate it?*

*I can hear your outrage and can understand why you are
irate, but we need to look at this situation from a calmer
perspective.*

*Badgering the faculty member will not necessarily change
the situation. Instead, let's look at ways to de-escalate the
tension in order to find a resolution.*

*It wouldn't be prudent to pursue this conversation any further
until you calm down.*

*That is a powerful accusation. What proof do you have to
back it up?*

*Maybe you are upsetting yourself for no reason. Can we
discuss what has infuriated you?*

The school hears your concerns, but you need to reciprocate and listen to our concerns as well.

There is an old saying that you catch more flies with honey than you do with vinegar. I think you need to change your approach and tone if you want us to assist you.

There is no need for belligerence.

We take a hard line and a hard look at this type of behavior.

We understand how this affects you, but you must also understand that your words and actions are not helping the situation. We need to ask you to approach the school with a more neutral attitude. We know this may prove difficult under the circumstances, but you must trust us.

Your hostility is not helping the situation.

Your insistence on being correct is making the resolution to this conflict more difficult to negotiate.

Your intense passion is clear on this topic; however, the school district does not share your point of view.

Your remarks are brutal and uncalled for in this situation. If you continue, we may have to ask you to leave the premises.

Perfect Phrases for Dealing with Irrational Parents

If a parent becomes irrational with you, either in school or out of school, stay calm. It's best to seek help, but if no one is around, keep a firm stance and don't let on that you are scared. Here are some phrases that are useful if you should become trapped in this type of situation:

Violent behavior is not tolerated. Your actions could be construed as . . .

I am not a punching bag for your displaced anger. I am on your side and here to help [child's name].

I can see where your frustration lies, but in fact, the school's faculty is under no obligation to . . .

I can understand why you are being so hard-hitting, as this issue deeply affects you, but you may want to consider some alternative approaches, because your current actions are causing me concern.

If you or your child physically hurts me or a classmate, we will press charges.

Challenging the decision in a violent manner isn't going to prove . . .

Clearly, we have a squabble, and both parties have strong convictions; however, I suggest we agree to work through our differences in order to maintain an open line of communication.

Perfect Phrases for Dealing with Obnoxious or Violent Parents

Just as more violence is being demonstrated by students, there is also a rise in parent misbehavior. I have had parents come drunk to conferences and say disparaging things about their own children. A parent might even strike or verbally abuse the child in your presence as a show of authority. Remember that you are a mandatory reporter of child abuse and must document any such incident with the school for child service organizations.

The parent might also make remarks that are hurtful to you because the child shows you more love and respect. Parents can often become jealous of a teacher who is popular with a child, because the child doesn't share the relationship at home.

If this type of parent arrives in your classroom, just endeavor to hold your ground without causing any form of confrontation. Use your emergency button to call an administrator to the scene, for both your own and the child's protection.

At some point, all you can do is report the incident to the administration for further action. Don't ever keep that type of encounter to yourself, because if the parent is like that with you in a structured setting, you can only imagine what the child goes through at home. Stand strong with a compliment about the child for every derogatory term that may come out of the parent's mouth.

If an angry parent says, "She was an accident; I never wanted her. She's nothing but a headache," respond: "I can't believe how blessed I am to have her in class. She is intelligent. She tries to complete all of her assignments. She is polite. She is respectful."

If an intoxicated parent says, "What an actress. Give my daughter, that bitch, an Oscar," say in a concerned voice: "Is that alcohol I smell all over you?"

Then, press the button and call for an administrator. Be sure the incident is documented, and always think in the best interest of your student.

Not all situations are that out of control, fortunately. Nevertheless, a conference with a parent may go astray through no fault of your own because you are defending the child against the adult. You may do well by using some of the following phrases to counteract parents like the ones just described:

A more positive approach may prove more constructive.

Being loudmouthed and argumentative makes for a cantankerous situation, so may I suggest you take a few minutes to calm down and rethink your approach?

Belligerent behavior is not productive.

How do you suggest we combat the problem? It appears we see two different sides to the same child.

I am asking you not to be impolite. I am feeling a level of hostility. Let's not stoop to exchanging blows, as it will solve nothing and put us back further from combating the issue.

I can see that our ideas are clashing. Maybe it is better we postpone this meeting and agree to disagree.

Please refrain from using that language while in my presence.

This is not going to turn into a brawl. I would like you to be a little more civilized while we discuss . . .

This is proving to be a challenge.

Vulgarity is prohibited.

We know this is contrary to what you want to hear, but . . .

What good things do you see in your son/daughter?

What you are saying is both out of line and offensive.

Words/actions of that sort suggest a level of uncouthness.

Why are you so enraged? Can you define what issues with your child you are angry about?

Why are you so opposed to my assessment of your child?

I feel as if you don't like your son/daughter. Is something wrong at home?

Perfect Phrases for Dealing with Parents in Denial

On occasion, you will find that parents or colleagues are in denial regarding a particular situation. Although denial can serve as a mechanism to help deal with adversity, in these cases it is more likely to be used to avoid facing possibile negative consequences that stem from everyday realities. Many times, facing the truth is too painful for people, so they pretend it is not happening.

Parents are often in denial about what their children are doing, and teachers can be in denial as well. As teachers, we get to know students, and we want to believe the best about them, but that mind-set can be detrimental to our profession.

I have experienced denial quite often when explaining to parents that their child's change in behavior might be due to drugs, alcohol, an abusive partner, or a range of other dangerous activities. Some parents pretend to know and be "OK" with the information, some call me a liar or threaten legal action, and some even refute their child's involvement in an incident despite incontrovertible evidence, just because the facts are too painful to believe.

In another very common scenario, parents pretend that classmates made their child cheat, or they deny their child's involvement—even though the child openly admits to the deed. No one is immune to denial, but as teachers, we must work to overcome denial in order to best serve the child. If you encounter this type of situation, try these types of phrases:

Are you denying that your child was involved with . . . ?

Can we ask why you think the school would mislead you on this issue?

I notice you keep hinting at _____ ; could you clarify what you are trying to say with concrete examples.

Insinuating that we are _____ is counterproductive.

Is there a reason that you are refuting what is being said?

It appears as if you are in denial of the situation at hand.

It appears you are operating on a different playing field from ours.

It is always difficult to accept that our child may have been involved with . . .

It is difficult to discuss this subject at this time because you are beyond the point of reason.

It might be a more calming influence if we were to . . .

Manipulating the situation will be counterproductive.

May I suggest, to alleviate the tension, that we . . .

Moderation might be the answer.

Mutual concessions will need to be made.

Pretending it didn't happen doesn't change the fact that it occurred.

This disclaimer of excuses you are using isn't helping us to improve the situation for your child.

Turning down our proposal is your parental right, but it isn't in the best interest of your child.

Vetoing our recommendations would lead to . . .

Your actions are contrary to our perceptions of . . .

Your refusal to accept responsibility for _____ leads us to wonder . . .

Perfect Phrases for Dealing with Parents with Unreasonable Expectations

Parents who have unrealistic expectations tend to hurt the emotional and mental well-being of a child. Their stance often leads to unhealthy pressure, which the child cannot withstand. Teachers also can have unrealistic expectations, and some have been known to ignore special education plans because they don't "believe in them" despite state and federal laws.

Certain parents may feel that if they don't have expectations that their child will at least meet the "norm," the child will be academically deficient. Unrealistic expectations can set hurtful limits when the child, despite great efforts, cannot make the goal imposed by the parents. Parents' expectations frequently are in conflict with the child's capabilities at the present time. Having an unrealistic expectation to meet can cause severe damage to a child's self-esteem. Helping parents to set realistic goals that correspond with the developmental needs of their child is integral to the learning experience. In this pursuit, the following phrases can be an aid:

At this time, it is not viable.

At this time, the suggestion that your child can _____ is unfeasible for the following reasons . . .

Do you feel that you may be suggesting something that would be impractical?

I have to be up front: what you are suggesting is out of the question.

Immature statements are not going to help improve this situation.

It is an adolescent trait to . . .

It is improbable that what you are suggesting will happen. However, if it does, we will deal with the situation at that time.

It is naive to think . . .

It is unlikely that what you are saying will come to pass.

No goal is out of reach, but we must also be aware that there will be limitations that may prove to be hurdles to achieving it.

That particular goal may be unrealistic for [child's name].

The feelings are raw.

The suggestions are unable to be realized at this time.

This is unworkable for the following reasons . . .

We like to work with attainable goals, and at this time, what you are suggesting is unattainable.

What is being suggested is ineffectual.

What you are suggesting is impractical at this time.

What you are suggesting is not a viable solution.

What you are suggesting is unachievable.

Your suggestion might work in another district, but right now for us, it is impracticable.

Your suggestions are very good, but they are slightly idealistic based on our resources.

When faced with stressful situations, the parent supports his or her child by . . .

Perfect Phrases for Dealing with Indifferent Parents

You can lead a horse to water, but you cannot make him drink. Indifferent parents are everywhere. They care about their jobs, their appointments, their spa treatments, their personal lives—basically, about everything other than the child they are supposed to be rearing. It is almost as if the child is extra baggage or, the opposite, an accessory to their collection of things.

In order for it to be about their child, you have to make it about them, like it or not. It is pitiful that these parents exist, but the reality is that they flourish. Usually, these people have a weakness: time, money, substance abuse, a need for love, the job, or maybe vanity. In the majority of cases, upon meeting them, it is clear into which category they fall, so that makes it easier to decide which approach to take. Here are some simple suggestions to keep in mind when speaking with indifferent parents:

- Emphasize (even though they don't want to hear it) that it is about the child's needs.
- Show how their needs are best met when their child's needs are met.
- Imply that the child's welfare is at stake, because this makes them think: "Could social services be called for my

indifference toward my child?" Many parents think that DSS and other children services are called only for physical abuse, but that is not true. Other cases may be harder to prove, but they are easier to investigate when a teacher has expressed a concern.

- Never threaten. Just talk around the issue, with simple mentions of situations that could occur if the problem isn't addressed.
- Use open-ended questions to figure out where the parents are coming from, in order to understand how to proceed most profitably.
- Empathize with them, but keep putting the responsibility for missed deadlines and rescheduled meeting dates back on them, so that you can see whether progress is being made.
- Ask them why it appears to you as if they don't care about the progress of their child.
- Ask what expectations they have of the child and where they see the child in the next twenty years.

As the educator, you are the professional in this situation. You should and must be the first to recognize the indifference and bring it to light, even if your initiative is not well received by the parent, guardian, or administrator. As the teacher in the classroom, you must also determine whether the indifference is only school related. If so, is it only in regard to your class, or does it carry over to the student's other classes as well?

Before speaking with the parents, check with your colleagues to see if it is a pattern of behavior. It may ultimately turn out that the parent was simply having an awkward moment and that your initial impression was erroneous. You can use simple phrases such as the following as a feeler to determine how best to approach the situation:

Can you explain to me why you are unresponsive? I am curious: is it just an off day for you? Are there problems at home?

Good enough is not good enough. You should want more than so-so results.

How much time are you putting in helping [child's name] with his/her workload?

I am feeling that you are apathetic toward the situation. Can you explain to me why that is?

I am seeing unexceptional concern toward [child's name].

I am trying to avoid unfair judgments, but I am finding it hard to tolerate the indifference that you are demonstrating toward [child's name].

I could be wrong, but it appears to me that you don't seem worried or concerned about the situation that I have been describing. Is there a reason for this?

I feel as if you are slightly indifferent toward [child's name]. Am I wrong?

I must be misinterpreting what you are saying, because for a minute there, I thought you appeared unconcerned about what I have told you about [child's name].

Is there a reason I am sensing a distance between your role as a parent/guardian and [child's name]?

Is there a reason that you are unresponsive to what the school is telling you about [child's name]?

On a daily basis, what role do you play in your child's education?

Some parents are overly concerned, but I am finding you to be the polar opposite. Am I misinterpreting the situation?

There is a sense of coldness and a lack of concern. This unresponsiveness and apathy is not in the best interest of [child's name]. At this time, I think it would be prudent to call a meeting that would include us, administration, guidance, and possibly social services.

What are your expectations for the child? How do you contribute to these expectations?

What does a typical day look like for you? How does [child's name] play into your day?

What is it going to take to get you more involved in [child's name]'s education?

Who is assisting the child when you are not home?

Why is it that you show such a lack of interest toward your child?

You seem unconcerned and uninterested in your child's development. What can we do to help change this?

You seem unmoved by what I have said. Is that a fair assessment?

You sound unsympathetic toward [child's name]. He/she needs support from both the school and the home.

It often comes to pass that your original hunch about the parents' indifference toward their child is correct. Normally, the indicators of indifference include, but aren't limited to, the following:

- Blowing off what you are trying to convey
- Showing outright indifference to the situation
- Simply put: they don't care

If you are dealing with a parent who is clearly indifferent, you may have to take a stronger approach in order to compel the parent to care. Here are effective phrases that you may want to use or adapt:

Do you understand the impact of your indifference?

Are you aware of both the long-term and short-term effects of your indifference toward what I am saying to you about [child's name]?

Blowing off what I am saying will not change what is happening.

If you don't care now, the situation is only going to get worse over time.

Perfect Phrases for Dealing with Abuse

If you are an educator, you are required by law to report issues that endanger a child's health, welfare, or safety. In most states, teaching professionals who work with children in any capacity are identified as "mandated reporters" and are required by law to report suspected child abuse or neglect.

Even though you report the matter to your school, you should still report it to your state's department of social services, as you may have an incident in which the report is not passed on by the administration. About a third of the states make it mandatory to report, while others have different procedures.

As the teacher, it is your responsibility to find out your own state regulations, which supersede those regulations set out by an administrator in a court of law. While only a small percentage of reports turn out to be deliberately false, some cases become classified as "unsubstantiated." If you are told that your report was unsubstantiated, understand that it means only that there was not sufficient information regarding the allegation based on the state's legal criteria, and not that you were wrong for reporting a suspicion. For example, some cases are classified as unsubstantiated if no court action was taken, but perhaps other services (such as counseling) were provided to the child.

It is a disturbing truth that in the United States, the criteria for substantiation vary among states because there is no uniform national system for case reporting of child abuse. What makes it even more difficult is that after you report a suspicion, you rarely will be allowed to learn the results of the investigation, due to family and child privacy laws. However, if the case is substantiated, the child can be removed from the home by emergency or temporary services through the efforts of an early-stage investigator.

In some cases, the early-stage worker may help to implement a plan to leave the child in the environment, with a contingency that the home is monitored. For teachers, this can be the most uncomfortable situation, because children in this position feel as if they can't trust you, as they are still with the family but are now considered a "troublemaker" or "tattletale" of their household affairs. Moreover, some results from your report may not be to your liking, as the agencies are often underfunded and overworked. The federal government offers a helpful website for teachers and other people who suspect abuse. You can review commonly asked questions and other details at childwelfare.gov.

Most veteran teachers have seen child abuse in its many forms during their teaching career, especially in girls who wear long sleeves, dark glasses, or colored tights to cover the bruises in cases of physical abuse. Sexual abuse and emotional abuse, however, are much harder to detect, but not impossible. So, as the teacher, it is important to remember that you don't need to have evidence to report abuse; you just need to have a suspicion or belief based on your personal observations. Following are the minimum conditions a teacher must address when aware of the maltreatment of a child under one's license:

- Physical abuse
- Mental abuse
- Emotional abuse
- Sexual abuse
- Public health concerns

In cases in which you suspect that abuse may be taking place, it is your obligation to intervene on behalf of your student. Abusive parents most likely won't come to your parent-teacher conferences, so you may not have the chance to address the situation directly. If you suspect something is wrong, it is best to refer the case to the district's administrative offices and the department of child protective services.

In 2007, the U.S. Department of Health and Human Services cited the finding that more than 3.3 million children were reported for alleged abuse just for the 2005 fiscal year. More bad news is that the violence these children see at home may result in their hurting others. According to federal statistics, more than 2,200 children have been sentenced to life and are serving in adult prisons around the country, and that doesn't include the thousands of children confined to juvenile detention centers until the age of eighteen or twenty-one. Therefore, to help ensure that you accomplish your purpose when reporting abuse, you may want to use the following phrases as guides:

Under my license, I am obligated to report . . .

I am a mandated reporter of suspected abuse.

In the interests of this child's safety, I am going to recommend . . .

I will be filing a Massachusetts 51A [or the number of the law in your state] that requires me to report to outside authorities on the care and protection of suspected abuse. . . .

I am going to suggest that the courts consider a CHINS [an order for a child in need of services or other state-equivalent acronym] for this child.

You could make a case for . . .

You have the right to contest my decision, but as a mandated reporter, I am filing _____ with . . .

I think the child's probation officer/social worker should be contacted.

The following incident occurred on [date].

I noted that . . .

Several people have reported that . . .

Attached is a photo showing . . .

Teachers who suspect abuse are constantly confronted with what-ifs. You may become more involved in a situation after initially reporting it, or be called to meetings or even asked to give testimony. Never feel that you are obliged to give someone an answer there and then. If you need time to construct your thoughts, ask for it. Answer only the question asked. Rumors, gossip, and unprofessional actions can fester in educational settings, and you do not want to be a contributor to that. Also, be aware of restrictions regarding what you can and can't comment on to people under federal and state laws protecting a student's privacy. Here are examples of what you you can safely say:

According to FERPA regulations, I cannot divulge what you wish to know.

I am sorry, but I cannot discuss this child with you. That information is protected under educational privacy acts.

I cannot comment because of privacy acts.

I don't have permission to speak with you about this matter.

If you feel this strongly about what you are saying, I'd prefer not to be involved, but you are free to call a meeting with the guidance counselor, the administration, and/or the child's family.

You might want to recheck your facts and talk to knowledgeable parties before commenting on this issue.

Chapter 4

Perfect Phrases for Homework and Coaching

Student coaching offers learners a jump start to increase their self-esteem in school by imparting both hope and encouragement. Teachers serve as academic coaches, providing professional instruction to help prepare students for their future. Drilling, tutoring, instructing, and teaching students through extra preparation and practice will have maximum effect when accompanied by positive support.

Your words serve as the foundation, if not sometimes a crutch, to brace the young learner through mastery of new curricula. As you cheer on and assist students, you are working toward greater collaboration and cooperation, which sustains and builds an optimal environment for learning.

Perfect Phrases for Praising Homework

Frequently, hours of homework are assigned to students, but when the assignments are turned in, they are not corrected in detail. As a result, a student who made multiple errors may never know it and may continue to make the same mistakes. Likewise, a student who performed exceptionally is not commended. Students are known to take advantage of a teacher's laxity by copying each other's homework, rushing through an assignment an hour before it's due, or not doing the work at all. Some teachers assign the same homework year after year, allowing the answers to be passed from sibling to sibling or neighbor to neighbor.

This section addresses positive feedback for teachers who diligently correct homework. Certain types of assignments must be checked with an eagle eye, while others may need only to be scanned to verify that the work was completed. In all of their day-to-day performance, students deserve at minimum a comment on the quality of their efforts. I suggest the following comments for those times when no in-depth analysis is needed. You'll discover that as much as a big red *X* can discourage students, these words can encourage students to do better or reward them for their attempts:

A++—superb job!

Awesome project!

Beautiful work.

Congratulations on a job well done.

Excellent first attempt!

Excellent work!

Fantastic project!

Fantastic work!

Good ideas, but you may want to organize them a little better.

Good job!

Good revision.

Good thinking.

Good work.

Great!

Great first draft.

Great style.

I like the words you chose.

I am impressed.

I hope to see more work like this from you in the future.

I like your idea.

I like your topic.

I see great improvement.

I'm impressed!

Impressive!

Interesting.

Keep it up.

Keep up the good work!

Much better.

Neat work.

Nice try!

Nicely done!

I can see you put forth a lot of effort—much improved!

Super!

Terrific.

This is clever.

This is done well.

This is excellent.

This is great.

This is well organized.

Very good.

Very nice.

Well done.

Well organized!

Well thought out!

What neat handwriting!

Wow!

You are creative!

The content of your work is original!

Your answers are correct, but your writing isn't so legible. Can you type or print your homework for me?

Your best work ever!

This is one of the best papers in the class!

You are becoming a superstar in math/language/history!

Perfect Phrases for Coaching Students

What does it mean to be a coach? Some coaches are into group hugs, and others would demean you for not making a goal. I have found that mentoring is usually the best approach. Being congenial and optimistic often helps people take risks and rise to challenges in order to hone their skills in a particular area.

Coaches typically relate to some children better than others. This is one reason why most children's teams have two coaches. Similarly, students relate better to certain teachers than others. Not every student is going to like your style, so as an educator, you must get past that issue. Make it a practice to phrase your comments so that they describe the work product and not the student. Here are some phrases that are effective to use with learners:

Absolutely what I was looking for.

Exactly right.

Excellent opening and conclusion.

Excellent work.

Expert work.

Good observation.

Good use of details.

I can see that you studied.

I like the way you have formatted your paper.

I like your draft.

I like your topic.

Keep mastering the information.

Once again, you are one of my rising stars.

Quality work.

That is correct.

That is nice work.

This is one of the best _____ I have seen.

Very convincing paper.

Very informative.

You are on target.

You figured it out.

You got it.

You have done well on this project.

You made a great start.

You must have put a lot of work into this project.

Perfect Phrases for Coaching to Promote Success

Coaching is a method of directing, instructing, and training students with the aim of achieving an academic or social goal. Sometimes it can lead up to the pupil's developing specific skills. There are many ways to coach, types of coaching, and methods for coaching students under your licensed supervision. As you are helping young people develop, it is important to coach students during their academic progression in order to further enhance their learning. Here are some neutral phrases that can coach students and offer them words of encouragement to promote future academic success:

Clear and concise work.

Excellent observation.

Excellent research.

Good going.

I believe in you.

I can see that you are turning it around.

I knew you could do it.

I like the way you have handled the topic.

I like your reasoning.

Impressive paper.

Nice choice of resources.

Outstanding.

That is a good point.

This is coming along nicely.

This is prize-winning work.

This is publishable.

You are on the mark.

You have written a well-developed theme.

Perfect Phrases to Motivate Students

Every experienced teacher knows that students will sometimes wait until the last minute to work on assignments. Even the period before your class, you might catch them copying someone else's paper. One way to motivate students to complete assignments properly and on time is to have a simple piece of poster board on display, with the parts of the assignment listed, so students can check off what they have completed or submitted. Students are competitive. They don't like to see empty spaces by their names, so, more often than not, they will do the work just to check off the box. With this type of motivation, students can become intensely involved in work that they originally didn't want to undertake at all.

Practically speaking, teachers don't always have time to come up with creative activities to motivate students, so an alternate approach must be taken. Here are some ideas for phrases to motivate students to complete work through segmentation:

Abbreviate the following . . .

Blueprint your ideas, and then find supporting facts.

Chart the following information.

Copy the information from the board.

Create a cartoon.

Create a project.

Define a single aspect of . . .

Depict what you are saying with more details and facts.

Diagram it.

Draw a simple picture.

Frame your argument.

Graph the data.

Hand in a draft.

Illustrate your point by . . .

In your report, offer us an accurate portrayal of . . .

Lay out what you want to do.

Map your ideas.

Note the following information . . .

Offer a brief description.

Separate the abstract concepts from the concrete details.

Outline the chapter.

Picture the moment in descriptive words and actions.

Plan your project.

Profile the person you are studying.

Represent the historical situation more accurately.

Represent your ideas, but make sure to document the sources of these ideas.

Shape your argument better.

Sketch out your thoughts before writing your paper.

Summarize the information.

Trace the lines.

Write a brief impression.

Write a synopsis.

Perfect Phrases for Student Reminders

For the student who needs constant reminders that work is due by a certain date, the following phrases may prove helpful:

Begin the warm-up activity board before the first tardy bell.

Bring the following materials to class every day.

Can you tell what is due this week?

Copy your weekly assignments into your notebook.

Don't forget to . . .

Don't hesitate to turn in work earlier than the due date.

Just a simple reminder . . .

Make sure to come to class on time.

Make sure to study.

Make sure you bring _____ with you tomorrow.

Make sure your parent or guardian signs your test paper.

Please remind your parents.

Put your assignments in your folder.

Remain in your assigned seat.

Remember, in this class, I expect you to . . .

Remember to tend to personal needs before coming to class.

Remember to turn in . . .

You must use the pass if you want to . . .

Your grade will be determined by . . .

Perfect Phrases for Classroom Reminders

On any given day, some students won't remember what you've told them either because they don't understand or because it has simply slipped their minds. If you want to ensure that your students acquire the information you impart, store it, and retrieve it at a later point, make it part of your routine to offer gentle reminders. Here are some phrases to help you remind students in your classroom:

Here is a heads-up.

How would you like me to handle this?

I am always available for extra help on these days after school . . .

I don't mean to hammer this information into your head, but it is on the state exams, so you must learn it.

I would like to inject some insights at this point.

Tell me what you learned.

Insert the missing information.

Inspect your work more closely.

Inspire yourself to go a step beyond the basic expectations.

Installing the software is necessary if you want to . . .

Instigating a conflict is not acceptable.

Instituting a new policy would be a great idea if you were to . . .

The interchange of information must be made clear.

It is important to guide the learner through . . .

Let's hit the books. Open up to page . . .

OK, you need to hold up until the rest of the class is finished with this section.

Please don't hang around in the halls, disturbing other classes.

Please don't hover over students who haven't finished yet.

There is no griping. This is not up for discussion.

Think about how what you have just been taught will influence your life.

We will work to help you reach . . .

Yes, you are correct; there is a hitch. If you notice, on page _____ , it says . . .

You may not hack into other computers using school-issued technology.

Perfect Phrases for Classroom Motivation

Motivational techniques in the classroom are similar to those used in the business world. First and foremost, you must hold students accountable. You must foster personal autonomy. Students must believe that you think of each of them as an individual. When trying to determine how to motivate a given student, depending on the age and home situation, there may not be a clear-cut best option. In any organization, some people are motivated primarily by fear, some by recognition, some by compensation, and, of course, some by natural ability or inclination for a particular field. The technique that has worked best for me overall is looking students in the eye and using their name before telling them what I need them to do.

You may well have to follow up in some form, since it is the nature of children to forget to complete work because something has distracted their attention. I have never seen an effective teacher who screams, yells, cries, or belittles students to control a class. It is better to use "gentle reminders." Here are some phrases that may help you motivate students either directly or indirectly:

Can I see you for a minute after class?

Can you come here and show me your work?

Can you partner up with [classmate's name]?

Can you practice with him/her?

Do you mind writing it down?

How did you do that?

How do you do it?

I am going to call on you next.

I am impressed with this.

I could see the hard work and effort you were putting in.

I know you will do it.

I really liked it.

I want to thank you .

Let's condense the information.

Let's look up this word.

Let's take a break.

Let's write the numbers together.

May I see how you are doing that?

Show me your contributions to the project.

Tell me what you understand.

Thank you for being on time.

This assignment isn't that long.

This should be easy for you to complete.

Well, they told me you could do it.

When can you find more time?

When you finish your work, you may put your head down.

Why don't you write to me about . . .

Will you be giving me more, or is this all there is?

Would you mind showing [classmate's name] how you did that?

You deserve a treat for your hard work.

You need to give yourself more credit.

You said you couldn't do it, and you did!

Perfect Phrases to Further Encourage Students

The home life of some students may not be desirable, and sometimes going to school is the child's safe haven for the day. It is important that, as the teacher, you strive to give students a positive experience in your classroom. At times, you don't have to say anything—all you have to do is offer a warm smile or a bended ear.

This section concerns the words that go along with those non-verbal cues. We are all human, and we like to hear the positives more than the negatives. Here are suggested phrases to further encourage students in your classroom:

Can I help you?

Can you repeat what you just said? People, listen up.

Congratulations on your certificate for completing . . .

Did everyone hear that?

Did I mean that? Of course!

Each of you will receive _____ if you . . .

Good illustration.

Good perspective!

Great picture.

Great! Can you tell the rest of us where you found the answer?

Hand in your proposal for your idea.

I am proud of this group.

I am glad you enrolled in this section.

I want to recommend you for . . .

I think you should apply for . . .

I hope you are in my class next semester.

I know you are going to get this.

I like your ideas.

I love your project.

I need more time to read this paper. It is really good.

I really liked what you did with this concept.

I think with your academic ability that you would be eligible to apply for . . .

I think you have such a positive attitude.

It makes me happy to see you smile. I am glad you are starting to understand the materials.

I want to give you this certificate because you completed . . .

I would like to call your parents/guardians and tell them what a wonderful job you are doing.

I would like to take you on a field trip.

I would love to learn how you did that.

It is clear that you study every day.

It is just what I wanted.

It's almost time to go, and I don't want to leave, because you have been a fantastic class.

Let's start from the beginning.

Let's stay focused. How about if we start back at this point and work our way forward?

How does doing it this way make you feel? [Some students need to be asked because tasks can throw them off depending on the mood swings or disabilities.]

Make it your voice.

Make sure you copy your assignment off the board. I am really interested in what you are going to do with this problem.

Neat poster.

Never lose hope! This is a valuable lesson for all of us—I had hope for you, and you delivered on it.

These projects are amazing!

Once I read your paper, I just knew the amount of thought you put into it.

Show me what you learned.

Show me what you want to do.

Superb answer!

Tell me what you were thinking.

Thank you for sharing that.

That is a great example.

That was a hard example, and you got it! Good job!

That was tough material. I am impressed with the way you tackled it.

Think a little more.

This is a good sentence.

This is the way to look at it.

This material isn't easy, but I will do my best to help you master it.

We have to finish up.

We can work on this together.

We will complete it in class.

What do you think? I am really interested.

What do you think is the cause? I want to hear your opinion.

What is confusing you?

When you finish, put your books back, and you may talk quietly with your friends.

Why do you always know the answer? You must have been studying!

Would you copy your work on the board for everyone else?

Wrap it up, and we can work on it again tomorrow.

You are a natural.

You are learning new things.

You can borrow some from me.

You did this on your own? Good for you!

You get what you get, and you don't get upset!

You have just given me food for thought.

You have really grown.

You have shown real academic improvement.

You have shown so much improvement.

You have to be one of the best and brightest!

You make me proud to say I am your teacher.

You really have learned to work well together.

You really worked this problem out.

You should include this in your portfolio.

Your ideas are important.

You're right; I was wrong. Two extra points for you!

Perfect Phrases to Build Students' Self-Esteem

Part of a teacher's role is to build students' self-esteem. In performing this role, always consider the age of your audience. What you say to an elementary school student, for instance, may be misconstrued by a teenager. There may also be differences in the type of language you use. For example, a kindergartner may not understand abstract concepts in the same way a middle schooler would. By choosing the right words, you're building a social relationship with the student in a professional manner.

It is important that you not only impart knowledge of a subject but also credit students when they master it. This may mean elaborating on subject matter or repeating it to students who didn't fully understand the first time.

Also, remember your purpose for communicating. Being sensitive to students' needs helps to build their self-esteem because it demonstrates that you care. Here are some phrases for building up a student's self-esteem:

I am happy to see a smile on that face.

I like your chapter review.

I think you did a good job on your flowchart.

Your class deserves a party.

I wanted to say thank you. I noticed how you helped [classmate's name].

You artwork is beautiful. Have you ever thought of . . . ?

You are really talented.

I want to ask if we can highlight your work on the bulletin board.

You followed the guidelines of the rubric. Good for you!

I like how you designed your story map.

Great lab notes!

You really can break down word problems.

I got your homework, and it looks good.

Hey, I just finished grading your quiz. Good work!

I love when you debate in my class. You have a keen instinct that separates fact from fiction.

I would like to include you in our newsletter.

You will go down in history someday.

Remember me when you are famous.

Great use of your voice.

I like the way you incorporated the technology.

I am impressed with your computer skills.

You really created a great character.

Great story! Did you ever think about publishing it?

Chapter 5

Perfect Phrases for Report Cards and Other School Documents

A grade is nothing more than a teacher's evaluation of a student's work. Assessment of the evaluations used changes from country to country, with different equivalencies. This is why schools in different countries have standardized charts, rubrics, and weights to measure course and grading equivalency.

The bottom line for a teacher is this: how did you determine the grade? Once when I was meeting with the parents of a student, the mother complained to me that her daughter got a B in gym. She said her daughter had always dressed and never missed a class. She felt the daughter deserved an A. Her husband was laughing and said, "I have seen her at practices walking around without a clue. Take the B and be quiet about it." No dice. His wife remained adamant and intended to call the school.

When that call comes in, the teacher must be able to justify the grade recorded on the student's permanent record. It is essential to phrase the response carefully.

If you are questioned about the grading of an assignment, you had better be prepared to answer for it. Grading has seen the gamut of practices, and very few teachers grade the same way. I have seen teachers grade a few papers from a packet in depth and only glance at the rest. I have seen teachers use highlighters to indicate that they have "looked at" the papers but never leave an actual comment. I have seen teachers use peer correction. This mixed bag is a prime reason why grades get called into question. Therefore, it is to everyone's advantage that you let students know how they are being graded.

Grades are a student's legal property. The principal has the right to change a grade as well as the legal responsibility to ensure the accuracy of the student's record, so any change should be put in writing. Let's look at the long-term picture: an inaccurate grade could have an impact on scholarships, awards, and college acceptances. For all of these reasons, my best advice is that you be as consistent as possible in your grading system and that you use a policy sheet to make your requirements or class expectations clear to all who read it.

Perfect Phrases for Describing Types of Students

Students have an endless variety of personality traits and talents. Their cultural and extended-family backgrounds can cover the globe. Still, among this diversity there is plenty of room for commonality. Here are some general phrases that could describe individual students in a typical class:

The student stops others from behaving poorly.

The student welcomes constructive criticism.

The student works well with . . .

The student writes excellent thesis statements.

Your child can handle diverse assignments. This was most recently demonstrated by . . .

Your child can speak/write convincingly.

Your child completes assignments accurately.

Your child contributes fresh ideas.

Your child demonstrates a willingness to hear others out before making a decision.

Your child is able to go with the flow and adapts readily to any change in circumstance.

Your child is honest and trustworthy.

Your child is open to ongoing suggestions.

Your child is resourceful.

Your child is skillful. He/she can . . .

Your child makes peers feel comfortable to express themselves in group work.

Your child operates under the assumption that . . .

Perfect Phrases for Describing Student Work Habits

Students' work habits also can take a multitude of forms. As an educator, you will need to describe your pupils' academic progress in a classroom situation. Students may have developed the ability to self-monitor and control their actions to a large extent, but it is up to you to give your professional observations. In some school systems, a teacher's comment on report cards or progress reports is mandatory. Your remarks allow parents to better understand how their child is doing in school. Here are samples of how to construct your observations:

Accepts responsibility

Accurately spells weekly lists

Acts politely

Acts responsibly

Adjusts to differences in materials

Applies language mechanics

Applies spelling skills to everyday work

Applies writing process

Asks appropriate questions

Beginning to learn how to . . .

Can answer questions appropriately when asked

Can complete with adult supervision

Can complete with modifications

Completes class work on time

Completes homework on time

Completes work most of the time

Controls talking

Courteous and respectful to others

Creates original work and projects that reflect the materials being learned

Demonstrates an interest in independent reading

Demonstrates an understanding of what is read

Demonstrates and organizes skills

Demonstrates effort

Edits and revises work

Exhibits self-control

Focuses and sustains attention

Follows directions

Forms letters correctly

Grade reflects specialized instruction

Interprets written questions

Is consistent

Knows addition facts

Knows division facts

Knows multiplication facts

Knows subtraction facts

Listens to learn, and learns to listen

Listens with understanding

Maintains a positive attitude when dealing with materials that prove difficult to master

Makes good use of self-directed time

Needs more practice copying . . .

Needs penmanship improvement

Needs to finish assignments

Needs to further practice printing/cursive letters

Needs to practice focusing on the teacher without being distracted

Needs to turn in assignments in a timely manner

Observes school rules

Oral reading and fluency

Raises hand when seeking an answer to a question

Shows promise in the area of . . .

Stays on task for long periods of time

Takes care of property and materials

Understands the concepts presented

Uses meaning in context

Uses phonics

Uses problem-solving strategies

Uses whole language

Works cooperatively in groups

Works well independently

Works well with help from an aide

Works without disturbing others

Writes neatly

Perfect Phrases for Describing Emotional Behaviors

One of the most difficult observations a teacher must share with a parent is a child's emotional behavior. Behaviors that are acceptable at home are not necessarily acceptable in a classroom. As you may already have discovered, parents and teachers don't always agree that a certain behavior is problematic. In fact, the parents and the child might demonstrate the same questionable behavior. The teacher doesn't want to insult the parent, but honest feedback may be necessary to rectify the problem. Here are some tactful phrases that might be suitable to the task:

It is believed that the student is underperforming and has the potential to do better.

The child becomes frustrated when . . .

The child complains regularly of . . .

The child has a tendency to make up stories in order to manipulate situations.

The child has been faced with _____ and has responded by...

The child is not well adjusted.

The child is unhappy and has expressed this feeling by...

The student avoids the core issues at hand.

The student complains openly to anyone willing to listen.

The student has a tendency to act like a drama queen in situations that don't go his/her way.

The student cuts himself/herself. I have reported seeing the following...

The student displays an unconventional approach to solving problems.

The student does not contribute to class camaraderie.

The student fails to give himself/herself enough credit.

The student has a different way of looking at things.

The student has developed a reputation for...

The student has difficulties boiling down complex issues such as...

The student has difficulty distinguishing...

The student has filed a complaint against a faculty member.

The student has had trouble with the law.

The student has reported unsafe home conditions.

The student has shown racist behavior/gender bias.

The student has unrealistic expectations.

The student is a loner and tends to isolate himself/herself.

The student is an "issue spotter."

The student is constantly distracted.

The student is nonresponsive.

The student is not involved in his/her own learning process.

The student is often disappointed.

Perfect Phrases for Evaluations

This section clusters the highs and lows found in a particular evaluation range. These examples can help teachers to create rubrics that allow for consistent grading. Not all student work can be graded numerically. In some instances, descriptors may be used to show where a student falls within a standard deviation of measure. In some schools, the ranges are limited to the words *satisfactory* or *unsatisfactory*. In other schools, the ranges become more descriptive and a third category, *needs improvement* or *shows improvement*, may be added. Set forth here are different series of indicators that can be used by an educator to evaluate, assess, and measure student progress:

Sample 1
Well above the standard expected

Above the standard expected

At the standard expected

Below the standard expected

Well below the standard expected

Sample 2
Excellent

Very good

Good

Satisfactory

Fair

Unsatisfactory

Needs improvement

Needs significant improvement

Unacceptable/Poor

Below standard

Needs attention

Sample 3
Outstanding

Brilliant

Exceptional

First-rate

Admirable

Superb

Tremendous

Perfect Phrases and Descriptors for a Rubric

Here are sample words for each of twelve levels, or tiers, that can be used to describe students' work:

Tier 1
Great

Really nice

Super

Fantastic

Wonderful

Marvelous

Fabulous

Tier 2
High-quality

Good-quality

Fine

Decent

Respectable

Worthy effort

Tier 3
Acceptable

Suitable

All right

Reasonable

Tier 4
Fitting to the topic

Adequate

Better

Higher quality than expected

Better-quality work

Improved work

Tier 5
Enhanced by . . .

A cut above

Tier 6
Just

Reasonable

Fair-minded

Passable

Average

Decent

Moderately good

Fair to middling

Tier 7
Unacceptable

Substandard

Not up to scratch

Not good enough

Disappointing

Insufficient

Poor

Not acceptable

Tier 8
Improvement needed

Needs development

Step it up

Needs upgrading

Not enhanced by . . .

Less than perfection

No advanced progress

Little expansion

Meets bare minimum of expectations

Little change for the better

Deterioration in quality of work

Tier 9
Deplorable

Improper

Not on topic

Offensive

Objectionable content

Unacceptable

Undesirable

Deprived of . . .

Meager use of . . .

Impoverished of . . .

Weak

Feeble

Meager attempt

Bad

Inferior work

Scanty information

Deficient in the areas of . . .

Mediocre work

Insignificant information cited

Tier 10
Of very low quality

Low standards

Below standard accepted practices

Beneath student's ability

Lower-quality work

Less-than-acceptable work

Lower than expected

Not more than the bare basics completed

Tier 11
No notice of . . .

Lacks concentration

Isn't edited

No sources

Little thought was put into the preparation of . . .

Little or no awareness of . . .

Lacks consideration in the areas of . . .

Inattention to . . .

Distracting details

Carelessness

Inaccurate information

Lack of attention to . . .

Lack of judgment

Tier 12

Horrible work

Awful work

Terrible work

Atrocious work

Dreadful work

Inferior work

Complete rubbish [UK]

Perfect Phrases for Discussing Report Cards with Parents and Students

Here are some general phrases that are applicable for talking about grades:

After a grade has been closed, I will not reopen it or take late submissions.

Grades are confidential.

Grades are nonnegotiable in my class.

Grades are private and can be shared only with a very few specified parties.

Grades are subject to change.

Grades close on [date]. This means all work must be submitted by [date and time].

Grades will be based on portfolio review.

Grading writing assignments can be very time consuming. It is expected that you will not repeat errors; that is why drafts must be submitted with final projects.

Holistic grading is used.

I award a daily participation grade.

I award letter grades A, B, C, D, and F.

I cannot give you your grades; you must get them from your counselor.

I cannot release grades without written consent.

I have customized my grade book in the following manner . . .

I have sent out weekly progress reports.

I keep an electronic grade book. This allows me to know student results up to the minute.

I may also mark an assignment as ungraded.

I may assign letter grades, points, check marks, and pass-fail grades. Each is weighted, and a student's grade can be calculated at any time.

I print my grade book every week.

I will change the grade provided that you . . .

If parents e-mail me, I respond to the e-mail with the information about their child's grade(s).

If you note a difference between the grade recorded on the assignment and the one in the grade book, you must bring it to my attention within a week.

My grade book is always up-to-date.

My grade book is set up for point values, which are weighted.

My grades are determined by percentages.

My grades were changed by the principal. Only the principal can discuss the rationale behind those changes. I am not at liberty to . . .

Papers are returned in the fashion they are received.

Students can access grade books.

Students can access my comments as well as their grades by . . .

Students may submit the assignment by . . .

Students will be graded on alternative assignments.

There is a forty-eight-hour turnover for returning marked papers to students.

You are receiving a letter of warning about your poor grades.

You need to improve this grade.

Your final grade will be determined by the following criteria . . .

Your grades have made you eligible for . . .

Your parent must pick up and sign the report card.

Perfect Phrases for Documentation

The following phraseology can be used for academic documentation:

Based on the article . . .

Commentary can be found online at . . .

Court papers stated . . .

Create a time line of events.

Details were added in the comments section.

Document all pertinent information.

Documentation is the process of producing evidence; anecdotal information should not be included.

Electronically file data.

Established policies and procedures . . .

File information that you think we will need at a later date.

File a grievance.

Filed data in student records are protected under FERPA.

Follow up.

Forward an e-mail.

Give details.

Give proof of . . .

Grade books must be kept on record for _____ years.

Have stamped.

Information is missing in the student's file.

The information was conveyed.

Jot down . . .

Keep a folder of . . .

Keep a record of . . .

Keep count of . . .

Keep track of . . .

Log in to/out of the computer lab.

Make note of . . .

Medical records confirm . . .

Minutes of the meeting were drafted . . .

Note down . . .

Original copies are available at . . .

Parental letter of consent is needed.

Photocopy of _____ must be on file.

Provide evidence of . . .

Put in writing . . .

Record what you observed.

Record your grades both on paper and electronically.

Records were compared . . .

Report to . . .

Send the _____ by certified mail.

Statements were made that suggest . . .

Student and/or parent must confirm . . .

The student must account for . . .

Student records indicate . . .

The student's paperwork must be authenticated.

Substantiate the following . . .

Teacher comments in the past have included . . .

Testimony indicates . . .

Transcripts are available through the guidance office.

Validate your facts.

Witnesses to the incident reported . . .

Write down what happened.

Write up an incident report.

Perfect Phrases Used for Testing and Measurement

This section will help teachers explain testing both in the classroom and on high-stakes examinations. These phrases may be relayed to teachers from testing companies or may be relayed to a district about a particular group of test takers.

Acting upon the recent results, we have chosen to . . .

Adjusted scores are cusps of point averages.

Allocated test sites will be located at . . .

Applied theory suggests that these tests . . .

Budgeted for _____ , the tests will cost the district _____ .

Compared with the _____ test, this test will . . .

Computed scores are reported by . . .

Corresponding items were scored by . . .

Created by a team of testing experts, pilot questions were introduced but were not counted in the score.

Documenting the results of the scores in student records will allow for . . .

Established testing practices require us to . . .

Forecasted results show that our school scores were in the _____ percentile.

Founded in part by _____ , the test was derived from . . .

Improvised questioning allowed us to use psychometrics in a new way by . . .

Information on a test can be interpreted to . . .

Interpreted scores tell us . . .

Introduced to new material on the test, the student performed . . .

Introducing the formatting process of testing often helps improve test scores.

Inventoried answer banks show us areas for improvement.

It is estimated that student scores will offer us the following feedback . . .

Negotiating test response items . . .

Originated from _____ , the test came into being in order to evaluate . . .

Presented to our school department, this test seeks to assess a student's ability to . . .

Presented with the scores, the district has decided to . . .

Presented with the scores, we have chosen to . . .

Publicized scores have led to . . .

Pursuant to reviewing the scores, we have decided to . . .

Quantified scores help to evaluate . . .

Recorded materials were used in the testing process.

Retrieved information was saved from the online portions of the examinations.

Solicited comments to improve test scores indicate . . .

Spoken words are often forgotten; please send testing concerns in writing to . . .

Standards are implemented not only on a local level but also on the state and federal levels in order to comply with the rules of No Child Left Behind.

Standards-based assessment allows us to mirror the test with what is being taught based on the frameworks of the curriculum.

Students receive _____ , composed of random items chosen from a data bank.

Students taking the test are encouraged to . . .

A test score will be clarified.

Perfect Phrases for Reporting Purposes

Teachers often need precise phrases to explain how a student is being evaluated or assessed. Here are common explanations you can offer to a parent or guardian:

Accommodations are being made to . . .

Accountability is assessed by . . .

Achievement tests were implemented.

Alignment with the curriculum makes our tests valid.

Alternate, alternative, and authentic assessments are used for performance-based evaluations.

Alternative assessment is available to eligible students.

Aptitude tests can be requested.

Assessment lets us know how the student is progressing.

Authentic assessment allows us to evaluate . . .

Benchmarks serve as our performance standards.

Content standards are necessary because . . .

Criterion-referenced testing is used by the district solely to . . .

Developmental assessment is completed during _____ or after . . .

Documentation is required to identify . . .

Early-learning standards are adhered to because . . .

Evaluation of your child is needed to . . .

Formal assessments are carried out throughout . . .

Indicators show that student performance has . . .

Informal assessments are offered to help students prepare for . . .

Norm-referenced testing is used when the school needs to determine . . .

Observational assessment can be requested by . . .

Outcomes are published regularly. Copies may be sought by . . .

Performance standards are used to benchmark our progress and our programs.

Portfolio assessment is required by all students to keep an ongoing record of progress.

Program standards are determined by . . .

Readiness tests help the district to make decisions on . . .

Rubrics are used to ensure fairness in grading and evaluating students.

The scores are counted if . . .

Screening is offered free of charge to all students who are eligible.

Standardized testing allows us to validate our programs.

Test results indicate . . .

Translated into lay terms, the scores indicate . . .

The verified scores can now be made public to parents.

We have advocated for . . .

Chapter 6

Perfect Phrases for Subject-Specific Report Cards or Homework

As a complement to the suggestions in Chapter 5, this chapter offers teachers perfect phrases for subject-specific report cards and homework. Specific content is necessary to show the extent to which a student is making progress in a core subject. Subject-specific comments allow parents to better understand what materials their child has mastered during the school year.

It may be the case that some students can be waived from courses based on disabilities. In those instances, it is advisable that an administrator dictate the phrasing for the report. Moreover, you want to make sure your wording meets the local school committee's and board of education's policies.

This valuable chapter offers you perfect phrases for the major discipline-specific areas that you may be assigned to instruct, including English and language arts, science, math, computer-aided learning and technology, general health and physical education, social studies, history, foreign languages, general fine arts, and music.

Perfect Phrases for Content Subject Areas

Along with remarks regarding individual students, certain statements can be made that are more generic, such as to describe the curriculum or classroom experience. You'll encounter example phrases under the various subject headings in this chapter. Here are some that fit multiple disciplines:

In this class, students are trained to . . .

The child was instructed to . . .

The learners have become skilled at . . .

The learners have gained knowledge of . . .

The learners were tutored in . . .

The pupils are trained in . . .

The student has been an active participant in the discovery process.

The student has studied . . .

The student was taught . . .

This course educated the student on the topic of . . .

This lesson satisfies [state/county] education standards.

Using appropriate language and formats, the child can . . .

We coached the students to improve their skills in . . .

What will be learned and why it is useful: . . .

Perfect Phrases for an English and Language Arts Curriculum

If you teach the core subject ELA, or any matter related to ELA, these are some choice phrases that you can use to describe a student's progress to a parent or an administrator:

Student has achieved a sound understanding of . . .

Student can readily explain the main ideas in the books he/she reads.

Student continues to read with enthusiasm.

Student has continued to develop skills in making accurate observations.

Student has well-developed interpersonal skills.

Child could improve his/her vocabulary by . . .

Interpersonal development requires that . . .

Student completes exercises and answers.

Student follows directions.

Student has gained vocabulary strength.

Student has shown vocabulary-building progress.

Student has strengthened his/her word power.

Student understood word roots.

Student uses defined words in context.

Student thinks through ways to use materials creatively.

The child can keep an audience's interest.

The child can locate and select information effectively from a range of sources.

The child can predict what might happen next.

The child has demonstrated the ability to speak clearly.

The child has learned to work positively with others.

The child has more accurate punctuation.

The child is beginning to use a wider range of kinds of sentences.

The child needs to continue to develop skills in . . .

The child needs to improve his/her punctuation.

The student continues to widen the range of sentence structures used.

The student does not hand in assignments on time.

The student has a good grasp of English grammar and sentence structure.

The student has a strong use of tenses.

The student has developed word power.

The student is good at analogies.

The student is good at reading books that contain abstract thoughts.

The student is good at understanding relationships in stories.

The student is intuitive.

The student needs to focus on planning before beginning work.

The student provides reasons for the ideas presented.

The student regularly completes the book's exercises.

The student's current vocabulary strength ranges from _____ to _____.

Perfect Phrases for a Science Curriculum

If you are teaching a science-based course, you can use the following phrases to discuss target objectives:

Student is able to use this knowledge to explain the properties of . . .

Student is skilled in designing experiments to test simple . . .

Student research project was well presented and clearly showed that [child's name] can . . .

[child's name] is able to work effectively with others to complete group tasks.

Interpersonal development in group work on experiments results in . . .

Student can mix chemicals.

Student can work with variables.

Student uses appropriate lab gear.

Student can dissect.

Student can identify animal parts.

The child can appreciate scientific principles.

The child can keep an audience's interest in his/her science project.

The child can predict what might happen next in the experiment.

The child can proceed through an experiment in logical sequence.

The child doesn't ensure that data support conclusions.

The child is defiant about course content based on religious beliefs.

The child is systematic.

The child needs to continue to develop skills in . . .

The student can collect data.

The student can make precise measurements.

The student can measure accurately using equipment.

The student can report data.

The student can separate fact from opinion.

The student can use and create a controlled atmosphere.

The student can use technical . . .

The student can work with abstract scientific concepts.

The student comes prepared to lab.

The student completes science projects.

The student does not like having physical contact with specimens.

The student enjoys chemistry.

The student enjoys earth science.

The student follows directions in science class.

The student follows safety procedures in science class.

The student has completed the science project with a mark of _____ for the work.

The student has kept up his/her science portfolio.

The student has memorized the periodic chart.

The student has participated in an outside field experiment.

The student has proved his/her hypothesis by . . .

The student is able to draw sound conclusions from observations.

The student is adept at the subject of science.

The student is an active participant in science-based discussions.

The student is disciplined.

The student is meticulous during experimental work.

The student is not interested in drawing conclusions based upon scientific principles.

The student is orderly.

The student is unscientific in his/her findings.

The student keeps up on current events in the scientific arena.

The student looks for exact findings.

The student looks into different possibilities to draw conclusions.

The student misinterprets data.

The student researches topics.

The student takes appropriate notes in science class.

The student understands basic scientific principles as they apply to . . .

The student understands how to take lab notes.

The student understands the scientific disciplines and their relationships to . . .

The student uses methodical approaches.

The student is systematic.

The student performs experiments haphazardly.

The student is a danger to others in the lab area.

The student is on task during science class.

Perfect Phrases for a Math Curriculum

Achievement in math, as in English, has to meet specific regulations and is assessed on standardized exams. The following phrases can help you to describe a student's progress in the academic area of mathematics:

[child's name] approaches math problems by . . .

Understands angles and degrees.

Algebraic problems are of interest to the student.

Arithmetic is [child's name]'s favorite subject.

Arithmetical work has proved difficult for the student.

Can use prime and composite numbers.

Numerical averages indicate that the student has . . .

[child's name] can compare quantities with relative ease.

The child can work with money to total sums and give back change.

Random mathematical problems seem to spark the student's interest.

Student can use different formats.

Students will understand area problems.

The child can count.

The child can make the following calculations: . . .

The child can manipulate geometric shapes.

The child can total numbers.

The child can understand basic absolute value.

The child can use statistical evidence.

The child has shown improvement in ability to count.

The child is able to accurately use a range of numbers.

The child is systematic in his/her mathematical approaches.

The child needs to continue to develop skills in . . .

The child understands accumulation.

The child understands incomparable quantitative comparisons.

The child understands the concept of whole numbers.

The child understands the concepts of money.

The pupil can use integers.

The student can add and multiply fractions.

The student can apply math principles to practical aspects of basic life functions.

The student can average numbers.

The student can count numbers.

The student can do fractions.

The student can draw angles.

The student can draw conclusions from similar patterns.

The student can find the mean, the mode, and the median.

The student can graph information.

The student can measure lengths.

The student can now add and subtract numbers to . . .

The student can subtract single-digit, double-digit, and _____ numbers.

The student can tally . . .

The student can understand hypotheses.

The student can use a formula.

The student can use parallel lines.

The student can use percents.

The student can use scales.

The student can use the order of operations.

The student can use the units of measure.

The student can use variables.

The student can work with angles.

The student can work with theorems.

The student does not self-correct mathematical errors.

The student doesn't carefully work out problem sets.

The student is able to define a point.

The student is able to do addition.

The student is able to draw sound conclusions from observations.

The student is able to plot.

The student is able to understand word problems.

The student is versed in times tables.

The student just chooses random answers without trying the problem.

The student repeats the same mistakes in the following math concepts: . . .

The student takes accurate measurements.

The student understand the basic geometric shapes of . . .

The student understands long division.

The student understands math as a discipline.

The student understands shaded area problems.

The student understands statistics.

The student understands the concept of rational numbers.

The student understands the concepts of the orders of operation.

The student uses decimals.

The students are being introduced to quadrilaterals and other polygons.

Perfect Phrases for Computer-Aided Learning and Technology

Technology is growing as online and distance-learning programs expand. Teachers often sign up their classes to use the school's computer lab to conduct research or interact with live feeds from the Internet. Even foreign languages are being taught using freeware from computer sites that allow downloads. Here are some phrases to show how to implement computer-aided learning and technology in your curriculum:

Student is actively involved in computer-aided instruction through . . .

Appropriate search engines are used in computer class.

Our grades are kept on PowerBook [or other program]; this allows students to access . . .

Our school uses the intranet instead of the Internet for the following reasons: . . .

The child can use a processor.

The child forgets to turn off his/her computer.

The child has been using the following programs in class: . . .

The child has learned the basics of a mainframe.

The child has learned the programming languages of . . .

The child has mastered the computer machinery.

The child has missed assignments because of technical problems with electronically submitted work.

The child has the computer know-how to . . .

The child has used a central processing unit.

The child is able to choose appropriate search engines on the Internet.

The child is able to safely and accurately use a range of computer programs.

The child is able to use computers to perform AutoCAD [or other program] functions.

The child is skilled in the areas of . . .

The child keeps up his/her workstation.

The child likes using the following software programs: . . .

The child likes working with computers because . . .

The child needs to make sure to regularly review his/her level of understanding of the work.

The child opens more windows than is permitted and tries to close them when the instructor walks by the workstation.

The child participates enthusiastically in team problem-solving activities.

The child seeks assistance when needed.

The child shows satisfactory use of a computer in the classroom.

The child understands CPUs.

The child understands the possibilities for using a supercomputer.

The child's strengths in the realm of computers ranges from _____ to _____ .

The computer has aided the student in grasping the following concepts: . . .

The student can capture a screen.

The student can do advanced searches very quickly to locate specific information.

The student can erase information.

The student has been caught hacking computer information.

The student can use a notebook.

The student can use the keyboard.

The student can use voice-recognition software.

The student can use Word and Excel.

The student has a good grasp of how to use technology.

The student has abused computer privileges.

The student has brought food or other prohibited items into the computer lab.

The student has harassed another student via the Internet.

The student has been caught illegally downloading materials.

The student has copied Internet materials and tried to submit them in class.

The student has submitted electronic work to e-publishing sites.

The student has used a laptop to ...

The student has used computers to create screenplays.

The student has used the Internet to research ...

The student is able to copy, cut, and paste.

The student is able to work well above the standard expected in instructional content and technology.

The student is familiar with both a Mac and a PC.

The student listens attentively to the ideas of others.

The student prints out appropriate materials.

The student remembers to bring his/her microphone and headset to computer class.

The student remembers discs needed for class projects.

The student remembers his/her memory stick.

The student sends texts or e-mails in class.

The student stays on task in computer class.

The student use computer-aided learning to master the subject of . . .

The student uses a laptop.

The student uses computer-aided language-learning software to . . .

The student was allegedly involved in computer sabotage.

The technological expertise of the child is . . .

The use of computers has helped your child to . . .

The usage of the software on the school's computer network has been . . .

Money has been allocated for a grant to expand our current technology program.

Perfect Phrases for a General Health and Physical Education Curriculum

Physical education programs are fairly standardized, and students in all regions have to meet certain requirements. However, the same cannot be said for general health classes. For example, some states use available resources to fund state abstinence programs; others fund or promote safer sex practices. The sample phrases in this section must be adapted to the regulations set forth in your state's guidelines or frameworks:

Student is involved in sports competitions.

As a sportsperson, the student is drawn to . . .

The child has participated in . . .

The child refuses to participate in . . .

The child will participate in the school play-offs.

The pupil attends sporting events.

The student can balance.

The student can fake opponents out with his/her athletic ability.

The student can hop.

The student can make a basket.

The student can manipulate obstacle courses.

The student can roll.

The student can run.

The student can take part in more activities.

The student does not fully participate in the gym course.

The student doesn't like physical activity.

The student doesn't line up.

The student doesn't pass the written exams for courses offered in gym.

The student doesn't pay attention to the directions for the sports lesson.

The student dresses for gym.

The student enjoys riding scooter boards, racing, and . . .

The student enjoys sports.

The student excels at games that involve . . .

The student excels in . . .

The student gives minimal effort in class.

The student has developmental issues that sometimes interfere with his/her ability to . . .

The student has difficulty mastering . . .

The student has mastered basic movement patterns and skills.

The student has produced a poster that shows a close understanding of . . .

The student has successfully led a small group of classmates to set up a team.

The student has the ability to do better in individualized sports versus team sports.

The student has trouble tumbling.

The student is a natural athlete.

The student is a team member.

The student is able to dribble a ball with satisfactory marks.

The student is actively involved in athletic competitions.

The student is aggressive toward others in competitive sports.

The student is agile.

The student is consistently late for gym class.

The student is fit.

The student is good at team sports.

The student is good in large-scale obstacle courses.

The student is in poor physical condition.

The student is nimble.

The student is often unprepared for gym.

The student is physically disabled and therefore, for medical reasons, was unable to participate.

The student is recommended for remedial work in the areas of . . .

The student is sporty.

The student is uncomfortable changing for gym.

The student is unfit.

The student is a competitor.

The student is in good shape.

The student knows when he/she is out.

The student maintains a positive attitude.

The student needs to improve muscular strength.

The student panics when involved in . . .

The student plays on extracurricular teams.

The student selfishly plays the games without consideration for others on the team.

The student shows vigorous attempts to improve skills.

The student talks in class.

The student understands tagging and sitting down.

The student uses the fitness center.

The student wastes time in the locker room.

The student will increase his/her fitness level.

The student wins and loses with good sportsmanship.

Thinking process and developmental skill range can be at odds when student is at play.

To maintain a healthy diet, it is recommended that the student . . .

When playing tag, the student understands what it means to be "it."

Perfect Phrases for a Social Studies or History Curriculum

To describe a student's mastery for reports in your social studies or history courses, use phrases from the following list:

The student can discuss civic duties.

The student can recognize our national symbols.

Students can listen to and read folktales and true stories from America and from around the world.

The student is knowledgeable about major historical events, figures, and symbols related to the United States and its national holidays.

Drawing on information from _____ , the student has demonstrated proficiency in . . .

The student has mastered _____ by drawing on information from local historic sites, historical societies, and museums.

The student can discuss five major concepts: location, place, human interaction with the environment, movement, and regions.

The student can analyze the causes and consequences of the industrial revolution and America's growing role in international relations.

Student can discuss the allocation of scarce resources and the economic reasoning used by government agencies.

Student understands the voting process.

Student grasps the overlapping themes of . . .

Student can address the origins of democratic principles . . .

Student can identify sequential actions such as first, next, last, in stories and use them to describe personal experiences based on historical experiences.

Student can show the meaning of the following historical concepts . . .

Student can identify temporal sequences such as days, weeks, months, years, and seasons.

Students can correctly use words and phrases related to time (now, in the past, in the future) and recognize the existence of changing historical periods (other times, other places).

Student is able to define and locate the . . .

Student is able to define and give examples of . . .

Student can locate continents, regions, and countries.

The student understands the meaning of time periods or dates in historical narratives.

Student can observe visual sources such as . . .

Student can understand directions, map scales, legends, and titles.

Student can identify and describe unique features of . . .

Student can compare maps of the modern world with historical accuracy.

Student is able to explain the structure of . . .

Describing the earliest explorations of _____ , the student can . . .

Student understands the responsibilities and powers associated with major federal and state officials, such as . . .

Student can identify the key issues that contributed to the onset of . . .

Student is open to different political views.

Student understands early American history.

Student can explain the rise and fall of . . .

Student can describe a _____ government.

Student can describe how _____ influenced . . .

Student can define markets.

Student can write narratives about historical figures.

Students can discuss courses of action when referring to . . .

Student can map . . .

Student can debate a political argument.

Student is able to conduct research related to historical topics.

Student can identify sources of conflict.

Student understands the psychological impact of . . .

Student can identify key figures, facts, and people.

Student understands the transitions and time progression of . . .

Student understands world politics and current events.

Student is able to present oral and written materials about ...

Student is able to explain in depth ...

Student can explain the reason for ...

Perfect Phrases for a Foreign Language Curriculum

Instruction in a foreign language is an integral part of a curriculum because students learn to communicate with other communities of the world. Teachers need to be able to describe a student's acquisition of the target language. The following phrases indicate various levels of student performance in the area of foreign languages:

Student is weak in syntax.

Student has trouble learning vocabulary.

Student is strong in the skill area of writing.

Student acquires languages easily.

Student has a phonological grasp of sounds used in the language.

Student can use declensions.

Student uses proper grammar.

Student grasps the mechanics of the language.

Student can make the appropriate sounds.

Students can write and speak in sentence form.

Student is a false beginner.

Student is recommended for the next course of study.

Student entered an immersion program.

Student is in a sheltered immersion program.

Student has difficulty grasping language concepts.

Student uses computer-aided language-learning software.

Student has difficulty reading in the second language [commonly referred to as the L2].

Student shows signs of illiteracy in the first language but is adapting in the second language.

Student has shown progress in the area of listening comprehension.

Student can converse fluently in the target language.

Student doesn't easily master the irregular verbs.

Student has difficulty with vocabulary.

Student translates concepts from the first language to the second language.

Student use inappropriate slang in the language classroom.

Student can mimic sounds.

Student can interact with media in the language classroom.

Student regularly attends language lab.

Student prefers dictation.

Student needs language repetition.

Student works better with the use of visual aids.

Student has nativelike fluency.

Student refuses to try to speak in the language.

Student understands the culture.

Student attends after-school language classes.

Student can ask and answer basic questions in the target language.

Student can translate texts.

Student has _____ oral and written skills in the language.

Student actively participates in speaking activities.

Perfect Phrases for a General Fine Arts Curriculum

Students gain a lasting appreciation of art forms through experience as a participant and as an audience member.

Students can increase their ability to express themselves in ways other than through spoken or written language.

The student can recognize many connections between the arts and daily life.

The student respects the uniqueness and creativity of himself/herself and others.

The student can express ideas using the unique languages of the arts.

Students can gain knowledge of the history of human creative achievements.

Students can develop insights into community and global issues explored by contemporary artists.

The student is proficient in the creative processes applicable to a variety of media, including technology.

Students can learn about themselves and others through critical reflection on their own work and artistic expressions from around the world.

Students can learn how societies and cultures construct and record their history, values, beliefs, and individual and collective visions.

The student can communicate through the arts using his/her imagination, ideas, observations, and feelings.

The student understands the contributions of the arts and artists to societies and cultures, past and present.

Perfect Phrases for a Music Curriculum

Music and the arts are the source of our country's creative spirit. A music curriculum helps students improve gross motor skills, creative thinking, and approaches to interpretation of patterns. Almost any teacher will tell you that special-needs children can be reached through the arts. Yet, much to the dismay of teachers, arts are often one of the first areas cut by district budgets. Parents with means can offer their children private lessons, but most parents can't afford a private musical education.

The following phrases are intended to help teachers describe student abilities in this field of study:

The student actively participates in school plays/musicals/theater.

The student can accurately transfer a rhythmic pattern from the aural to the kinesthetic.

The student can adapt to changes in musical patterns.

Students can alter the manner in which they are required to respond to the teacher or to the instructional approach.

Students can alter the pace of the lesson to ensure that they master the concept being presented or are being challenged by the presentation.

Students can alter the setting so that a peer may benefit more fully from the instruction.

The student can analyze the elements of works and describe memorable parts.

Students can change the materials in musical compositions to enhance rather than impede learning.

The student can combine expressive and structural elements of a musical style.

The student can compare and contrast the use of techniques in different compositions.

Student can perform advanced compositions.

Student can create desirable tone quality.

Student demonstrates accurate memorization and reproduction of movement sequences.

Students are encouraged to participate fully in both planning and instruction.

Student can evaluate a given musical work and determine what qualities or elements were used to evoke feelings and emotions.

Student can explain personal preferences for specific musical works and styles using appropriate terminology.

Student explores possibilities in nuance to achieve a wider spectrum of artistic expression.

Student can hear the beats.

Student can identify and define standard notation symbols for pitch and rhythm.

Student can identify and explain compositional devices and techniques used in a musical work.

Student can introduce attempts to increase rate of performance only when he/she has achieved a high level of accuracy.

Students can modify evaluative procedures to maximize the amount of relevant information received.

Student can monitor the use of vocabulary.

Student can read and perform whole, half, quarter, eighth, sixteenth, and dotted notes and rests in a variety of simple, compound, and complex meters.

Student can read notes.

Student can sing in tune.

Student can sing the scales.

Student can use computer software to create music.

Student can use expressive and structural elements.

Student can use interactive techniques that allow close monitoring of individual progress.

Student can use mathematical vocabulary to describe music.

Student demonstrates difficulty with . . .

Student has become proficient in the following areas of music theory . . .

Student has difficulty hearing sounds.

Student holds the correct posture with an instrument.

Student is learning how to play . . .

Student is recommended for the honors program in the arts.

Student shows expressive intent.

Student understands harmony, chords, and melodies.

Student understands stylistic characteristics.

Student writes musical scores.

Chapter 7

Perfect Phrases for Dealing with Student Discipline

One of the most important tasks that a teacher must perform is to document student discipline, as you are entrusted with the health, welfare, and safety of children. Today, most schools post copies of state and federal prosecution laws over the pay phone to discourage bomb scares, threats, or other acts that might cause terror or disruption to the learning environment. Against this backdrop, documenting student discipline has become serious business, particularly since the tragedy at Columbine High School.

Most districts require faculty to document incidents with dates and times on student personnel slips. Information on these slips is usually recorded in a database before or after being sent on to an administrator or a guidance counselor. The school usually returns a copy to the teacher that specifies the action taken by the school or administration. These comments are recorded on the student's permanent record and may result in suspension or expulsion.

Oral conferencing and written documentation are part of an educator's daily routine, especially as the students get older. Things can go amok in schools every day, and it is inevitable that you will have to respond to such incidents for multiple purposes through face-to-face conferencing, written documentation, and follow-up actions. The tools in this chapter are designed to help you with that task.

Perfect Phrases for Classroom Management

Classroom management can make or break a teacher. If you cannot control your classroom, it will be chaotic. Control doesn't mean that you are a drillmaster. Instead, you command a class the way a conductor leads an orchestra—with finesse, authority, and a soft touch to soothe the souls around you.

You should always start out on the strict end of the spectrum and loosen up on occasion. If you start out loose, you will most likely not gain control of your class for the entire year. Never let students see your weak points. No matter how stressful you feel, you need to remain as calm as you can be.

When you need a student to cease a behavior immediately, any of these relatively strong phrases may be in order:

Apologize now.

Break it up.

Close it now.

Desist!

Desist or face detention.

Do you want detention?

Don't continue with that.

Drop it.

End it.

Finish it up.

Halt!

Hand it over.

Hang it up.

Hold up.

Knock it off, now.

Put your brakes on.

Quit doing that!

Retract that.

That was uncalled for.

Perfect Phrases for Common but Unacceptable Behavior

On a typical day, a student may act out in a common but unacceptable manner through inappropriate statements or behaviors. Here are some sample phrases for you to use to document observations:

Doesn't seem to believe the rules apply to him/her.

The student maintains a blog that . . .

The student makes decisions without weighing alternate courses of action.

The student makes others feel intimidated and has indicated that he/she sees this behavior at home.

The student may be involved with risky behaviors.

The student never appears to sweat the details.

The student pits classmate against classmate.

The student rarely contributes to group projects.

The student has agreed to report incidents to faculty and staff after being bullied.

The student seeks out constant approval from peers.

The student seeks out negative attention.

The student shows poor decision-making skills.

The student shows signs of depressive behaviors.

The student speaks poorly of competitors.

The student speaks up against perceived injustice.

The student stands up for just causes.

The student defends his or her work.

The student maintains a positive outlook in times of adversity.

The student works for social change.

The student accepts and works well with others from more diverse backgrounds.

The student spends a good amount of time on personal matters instead of schoolwork.

The student uses pressure to unduly influence . . .

The student's humor affects classroom behavior.

The student's romance is interfering with his/her schoolwork.

There have been complaints in regard to . . .

Your child does not consistently think through his/her actions and words.

Your child does not lead by example.

Your child has a flash temper that comes out when . . .

Perfect Phrases for School-Based Offenses

Every school has a policy for reporting school-based offenses. Teachers tend to write either one or two words that simply label the situation, such as "Insubordination!" When you document a school-based offense, your account of the incident should answer the following questions:

- Who was involved?
- When did it happen?
- Where did it happen?
- What might be the reasons why it happened?
- How did it happen?

Teachers may write a narrative story instead of stating only the bare facts, but should not insert personal opinion, regardless of how tempting it may be to do so. Realize that what a teacher puts in print could someday end up in court. Here are some phrases to aid you in writing up an incident report:

Behaviors That Can Lead to Arrest, Expulsion, or Suspension

Aggressive and threatening language has been used . . .

Arson was committed by the student.

Attacking a teacher, the student . . .

The student requested sexual favors from . . .

The student detonated . . .

The student set a fire . . .

The student showed inappropriate physical conduct directed toward others.

The student threatened [classmate's name].

The student was abusive to [classmate's name].

The student was caught in the sale of . . .

The student was caught with firecrackers.

The student is bullying another student by . . .

The student is in the process of obtaining property from another with or without the person's consent by wrongful use of fear, threat, or force.

The student incited a riot.

Dangerous substances were found on the student.

Fighting led to the student's being injured and . . .

Fire alarms went off due to . . .

The student attacked another student.

The student has falsified records.

The student endangered himself/herself and others by . . .

The student had a combustible substance.

The student had a smoke bomb.

The student attempted to cause bodily injury to a classmate.

The student caused disfigurement to . . .

The student caused extreme pain to . . .

The student caused others discomfort.

The student conveyed threats of bodily harm.

The student has brought an object that is like a gun or firearm onto school grounds.

The student has physically attacked a staff member.

The student has used extortion.

The student hazed others.

The student is in possession of _____ , with the possible intent to cause bodily harm . . .

The student is involved in gang activity.

The student has been in possession of handguns, rifles, shotguns, and bombs.

The student risked the life of another student.

The student sexually assaulted [classmate's name].

The student possesses a weapon and has expressed intent to use it against another student.

The student showed evidence of drug use.

The student showed evidence of sale of [controlled substances].

The student was caught gambling.

The student was caught in a con.

The student was caught misusing materials for euphoric pleasure.

The student was caught spray painting.

The student was caught using alcohol.

The student was caught using inhalants.

The student was caught with alcohol.

The student was caught with intoxicants.

The student was charged with possession.

The student brought an explosive substance to class.

The student brought flares into the school zone area.

The student called in a bomb threat.

Behaviors That Can Lead to a Referral for Disciplinary Action

Classroom disruptions have increased since _____ because of the student's insistence on . . .

Disrespectful behavior was demonstrated.

Disruption by the student's actions led to . . .

Insubordination was documented by [name of witness] after the student . . .

The student cheated.

The student fails to comply with regulations.

The student fails to comply with school rules.

The student harassed . . .

The student has been caught cutting class.

The student has instigated . . .

The student has lied.

The student has posted inappropriate materials on the Internet.

The student has repeatedly over time interfered with a classmate through bullying or threats.

The student has shown academic dishonesty.

The student has used or displayed an object that is similar to a weapon or could be mistaken for a weapon.

The student hit [classmate's name].

The student ignored suspension codes issued by the school.

The student impaired . . .

The student incited a disturbance by . . .

The student interfered with another student's ability to participate in or benefit from . . .

The student interfered with the school's educational program.

The student intervened in a teacher's attempt to stop . . .

The student is defiant.

The student left school grounds.

The student made inappropriate comments.

The student made inappropriate physical gestures.

The student prevented the orderly conduct of . . .

The student pushed [classmate's name].

The student refuses to obey school policies.

The student skipped a school activity.

The student struck a staff member.

The student teased . . .

The student tried to sell look-alike drugs.

The student upset the class by . . .

The student was abusing over-the-counter medicines.

The pupil discharged a fire extinguisher.

The pupil gave false information concerning the placement of explosive or destructive substances.

The pupil kicked in a locker.

The pupil knew and conspired with the student who . . .

The pupil took or obtained property of another without permission.

The pupil turned over a desk.

Behaviors That Can Lead to Detention or Further Suspension

The student was assisting another student in . . .

The student was caught altering records.

The student was caught chewing . . .

The student was caught copying . . .

The student was caught forging a signature.

The student was caught rummaging through another student's bag.

The student was caught spitting.

The student was disrespectful.

The student was found in an unauthorized vehicle.

The student was found skipping class.

The student was involved in a fight.

The student was involved in an unwanted sexual advance.

The student was involved in the following disruptive activity: . . .

The student was involved in an altercation.

The student was unlawfully absent from a class.

The student was using tobacco products.

The student was walking the halls without a pass.

The student wore gang-related materials.

The student's clothing and hair is noncompliant with the dress code.

The student's poor behavior interferes with the learning of others in a classroom.

The student refused to follow directions of teachers.

The student had a dangerous weapon other than a firearm.

The student used intentional negative actions.

The students were in possession of drug paraphernalia.

The students were involved in the use of . . .

The student was not prepared for class. He/she didn't bring . . .

The pupil allegedly stole . . .

The pupil attacked a teacher.

The pupil broke glass.

The student cannot participate in _____ because of a punishment sanctioned on [date].

The student caused a classroom disruption.

The student caused a false alarm.

The student's clothing is disruptive to the learning environment.

The student has been given in-house for . . .

The student has been removed from extracurricular activities because of . . .

The student has detention as a result of . . .

The student has misused educational technology.

The student has visited unauthorized computer sites.

The student has put inappropriate materials in a school locker.

The student has used inappropriate language.

The student has used vulgarities.

The student interfered with the effective learning of . . .

The student is on academic probation because of . . .

The student is truant.

The student led a nonsanctioned protest.

The student made unwelcome advances . . .

The student misused school property by . . .

The student must attend _____ for _____ days.

The student participated in a disturbance by . . .

The student placed a phone call to _____ , which caused . . .

The student refused to participate in the lesson.

The student was in the act of distributing . . .

The student was involved in a confrontation with another student.

The student was involved in public displays of affection.

The student was involved in sexual activities.

The student was involved in the destruction of property.

The student was issued a warning.

The student was smoking.

The student is suspected of using drugs.

The student withheld information about another student regarding . . .

The student's behaviors disrupt the learning environment.

The student participated in an illegal activity outside of school hours in violation of the code of conduct.

Theft occurred and was reported on [date].

Behavior Concerning the Welfare of the Student

The student violated probation.

The student has run away.

The student has been missing for _____ days.

The student was reported to the Department of Social Services.

The student has been referred to counseling.

The student has been arrested for . . .

The student's parents were contacted in regard to the incident on [date].

Weapons are clearly prohibited, yet the student decided to . . .

The student was involved in a hate crime.

The student was involved in a gang-related incident.

The student contributed to the malfunctioning of . . .

The student was issued medical attention for . . .

The student needs protective services.

The student has been involved in vandalism.

The student showed inappropriate use of a toy.

The student destroyed a schoolbook.

Perfect Phrases for Disciplinary Measures

Sometimes the line of duty is blurred. The following phrases should probably come from an administrator, but in some systems, it is the teacher's interim responsibility to substitute for the administrator. These phrases address the most common disciplinary actions:

Your child has been expelled.

Your child has been recommended for alternative schooling.

Your child has been suspended.

Your child has received in-house suspension.

Your child shows sociopathic behaviors. Therefore, I am recommending a meeting with the school psychologist to diagnose if any mental illness may be the reason for your child's actions.

Your child was issued a demerit.

Your child was issued detention on the following date(s) . . .

Perfect Phrases for Describing Neutral Behaviors

Sometimes behaviors are neither bad nor good but still are worth noting in the official records, for a variety of reasons. The following phrases could be helpful in an assortment of situations:

Based on my experience, the student . . .

I was unaware that the student suffered from . . .

This placement was made by a state agency to an institutionalized setting for noneducational reasons.

The student is in a full inclusion program because . . .

The student is in a partial inclusion program for . . .

The team has identified that the student needs a substantially different classroom, separate day school, or a residential placement.

A doctor has determined that the student needs a home-based, hospital-based, or juvenile facility–based program.

The student has a satisfactory attendance record.

The student is undergoing medical care.

The student is unwilling to entertain ideas different from his/her own.

The student is well prepared.

The student isolates himself/herself.

The student listens to the teacher and responds appropriately at times.

The student's behavior shocked me at first, but now I understand . . .

Your child has trouble juggling competing priorities.

Perfect Phrases to Promote Positive Actions

Positive reinforcement must take precedence over negativity. Teachers must make an effort to use positive feedback. For example, instead of labeling something a "problem," which sounds negative, call it a "challenge," showing that the student can overcome the difficulty. An IEP report might read, "Bill's challenges with gross and fine motor skills have effected language delays that are now documented in social and academic areas." Then the school will most likely write a positive and obtainable accommodation to show how the student can progress to the next step, such as "Has been recommended for small-group language instruction and may be a candidate for Tier 2 reading intervention." Whenever possible, catch the student doing something right, as expressed in the following examples:

The child uses his/her imagination to . . .

Despite the fact that the student is undergoing medical care, all of his/her work is up-to-date.

The student acknowledges . . .

The student acts proactively.

The student appreciates and promotes diversity.

The student can solve difficult problems.

The student can speak persuasively.

The student comes to the class refreshed and ready to learn on a regular basis.

The student confronts issues or differences in a professional manner.

The student cooperates well with others.

The student demonstrates model behavior.

The student has rapport with . . .

The student has redefined his/her study habits by . . .

The student identifies . . .

The student is comfortable with . . .

The student is conscientious.

The student is dependable.

The student is logical.

The student is open-minded.

The student is rarely tardy.

The student is rational.

The student is tactful.

The student is well adjusted.

The student is well prepared.

The student is willing to entertain concepts different from his/her own.

The student listens to the teacher and responds appropriately.

The student shows initiative.

The student shows sufficient knowledge.

The student takes academic risks that pay off.

The student takes on challenging projects.

The student takes responsibility for his/her actions.

The student thinks outside the box.

The student turns work in well in advance of the deadline.

Your child exceeds in . . .

Your child is a pleasure to have in class.

Your child is one of my best students.

Your child shows great potential.

Perfect Phrases for Describing Improvement

The student has made progress in particular areas, but there still may be issues. Here are some helpful phrases to describe that status under various scenarios:

The student puts too much pressure on himself/herself.

The student speaks in vague terms.

Your child requires little to no direction.

The student is working toward more interdependence.

Your child has a thorough knowledge of . . .

I have watched your child improve in the following areas . . .

The student is progressing.

The student has demonstrated improvement.

The child has demonstrated academic growth.

The child has made dramatic improvements by . . .

The student has put forth great efforts.

The student is improving his/her accuracy.

The student is becoming more consistent.

The child has shown great progress since . . .

The data show . . .

Your child's ability to _____ has increased.

Your child has shown the ability to . . .

The student is meeting standards.

The student is overcoming challenges.

The student is building up his/her self-esteem.

The student is meeting national/state standards.

Perfect Phrases for Describing Lack of Improvement

Sometimes no improvement is noticeable, and the child is not progressing. The following are accurate educational phrases that can be used to describe a given set of facts; these may be helpful on report cards as well.

Student does not meet deadlines.

Student does not seek regular feedback.

Student fails to assume responsibility for his/her actions.

Student was caught stealing.

The child has tended to resist new assignments and work plans.

The child is maladjusted. This is demonstrated by his/her actions.

The student asks questions for question's sake.

The student attributes blame to others.

The student avoids acknowledging his/her errors.

The student bites others.

The student challenges standards, which has led to disruptions.

The student discourages others.

The student does not seek out creative alternatives to conventional practices.

The student doesn't appreciate diversity.

The student doesn't behave in accordance with the school's mission statement.

The student doesn't value peers as equals.

The student engages in shouting matches.

The student fails at punctuality.

The student frightens others by . . .

The student has been caught cheating.

The student has been caught lying.

The student has been caught using a cell phone during class time.

The student has been documented for having to be removed from class for inappropriate behavior.

The student has been insubordinate.

The student has been known to make numerous off-the-cuff remarks.

The student has been referred for disciplinary measures.

The student has been referred to the office.

The student has established a reputation for . . .

The student has hit other students.

The student has incomplete credits.

The student has not communicated information from the school to the parent.

The student has received a failing mark for plagiarism.

The student has served as a catalyst for problems, which have led to . . .

The student has thrown objects at others.

The student has trouble maintaining composure.

The student instigates problems.

The student is disrespectful to the teacher.

The student is inconsistent.

The student is misleading his/her parents about schoolwork.

The student is not committed to . . .

The student is seen walking the halls during class time.

The student is unable to communicate end results.

The student kicks others.

The student makes little effort to understand . . .

The student makes threats.

The student misses opportunities to . . .

The student needs to be the center of attention.

The student overlaps assignments.

The student oversteps the boundaries.

The student plays individuals to get what he/she needs.

The student shows minimal effort toward assignments.

The student tends to postpone doing work.

The student tends to use objectionable language in regard to people who are different.

The student uses defamatory language.

The student uses derogatory language to humiliate others.

The student uses vulgarities to express himself/herself.

Your child appears to be neglected in terms of . . .

Your child has little awareness of . . .

Your child is reluctant to confront . . .

Your child lacks goals.

Your child must constantly be redirected.

Your child uses age-inappropriate language.

Perfect Phrases for Describing a Safety Situation

This section deals directly with aspects of school safety and school climate. In a recent federal report, more than 66 percent of the nation's school resource officers polled indicated that their emergency plans were not practiced on a regular or ongoing basis. In general, districts and public schools should have a "shelter plan" that suggests where students should go for protection if a dangerous situation were to occur, along with a printed set of concise lockdown procedures.

Reports funded by the Bureau of Justice in Washington, D.C., estimate that in this country there are forty-eight violent crimes committed per one thousand students. Some 21 percent of our nation's schools reported having gang-related activity, and 33 percent of students polled said they were involved with a fight during their school years. According to the reports, theft averages change from year to year, with a range of thirty-eight to ninety-five out of every one thousand students being a victim.

Further, over the five-year period from 1998 to 2002, on an annual basis, teachers were the victims of approximately 234,000 nonfatal crimes at school, including 144,000 thefts and 90,000 violent crimes, such as rape, sexual assault, robbery, aggravated assault, and simple assault. More than 78 percent of school resource officers reported taking away a weapon from a student. According to estimates, a minimum of twenty-one homicides take place on school grounds each year. Meanwhile, 29 percent of school principals report bullying of students on a weekly basis. Perhaps even more sadly, in one report, 79 percent of students said that violence was caused by "stupid things like bumping into someone."

As an educator, consider this: at least twenty states allow students under the age of eighteen to open-carry handguns. What is more frightening is that an estimated 430,000 students (2 percent of all students) self-reported that they had at least once taken something to school to protect themselves from attack or harm. This reported "protection" included guns, knives, brass knuckles, razor blades, and spiked jewelry, among other objects.

All schools should have a policy outlining procedures to be followed in the event of possible emergency situations. Policies may need to be reviewed and updated on an annual basis. Some states require that a school district submit a published handbook of policies and regulations to the state for review and approval.

This section lists phrases that you may find useful to discuss and document common emergencies that occur in school districts:

Staff was called to a code blue.

Staff was called to a code red.

Staff contained students in a lockdown.

Students participated in an evacuation.

Students were taken off school grounds.

Student behavior led to an actual emergency.

Students were made to stay in a secured area.

Students blocked an exit.

Students encountered a blocked exit.

Doors and windows were closed before the fire drill.

Teacher did not take roster outside of building during emergency.

Students went into a lockdown mode.

Student refused to leave a classroom after an incident that endangers a staff member or students.

School was not in compliance with fire laws.

A smoke bomb exploded. As a result, the fire alarm was set off in the main office.

The following public services were contacted in a timely manner . . .

A fire was set in the building.

When the drive-by shooting occurred . . .

Only one main entrance to the school is in use during the school day, and visitors must be buzzed in.

All visitors must sign in at the office.

Two-way communication devices between staff and the building are in use when staff members are outside on school grounds.

Lockers were searched because . . .

Vandalism occurred.

Perfect Phrases for Documenting Situations Involving Other Teachers

A teacher should never, ever touch a child in a disciplinary matter. All of the behaviors here are completely unacceptable, and yet, according to statistics and personal accounts, we know that they happen. If you witness a fellow teacher or staff member engaging in any of the following activities, be sure to document what you see and report it to the administration at once:

- Belittle a student in front of the class
- Slap a student on any part of the body
- Make a student sit in the hallway or outside the building without supervision
- Throw a student against a locker
- Shake a student
- Punch a student
- Throw something at a student
- Pinch a student
- Remove an article of clothing from a student
- Watch while a student bullies another student
- Take a personal item from a student under the guise of "contraband"
- Empty out a student's locker without permission of the administration

A colleague who is guilty of any of the actions just listed has abused his or her power and position.

The following phrases address how to report a fellow faculty member for abuse, as well as how to speak with colleagues when their behavior disturbs you:

The teacher was verbally abusive.

The teacher was physically abusive.

The teacher administered corporal punishment.

Teacher denied student a lunch period.

Teacher caused the student to miss the bus.

Teacher issued a detention without due notice.

Teacher denied student due process.

Teacher has used extortion or blackmail tactics.

The teacher delighted in student punishment.

If I see this again, I will report you.

I need to report your actions to the office.

I have spoken to you before about this, and now . . .

I feel you're in collusion with the students. Is it true that . . .

It is in our policy that you are not to fraternize with students by cell phone or computer.

I feel you are closing your eyes to what is going on in . . .

I refuse to back your behavior toward the student because . . .

It has come to my attention that you have partied with students . . .

I am going to guidance based on my observations . . .

I know that the teacher is usually believed over the student, but I overheard the incident and . . .

Please don't talk about faculty members in your classroom.

What is discussed at a faculty meeting is not for general consumption because . . .

Chapter 8

Perfect Phrases for Dealing with Special Education Students

Did you know that when Congress enacted Public Law No 94-142 in 1975, it found that there were more than eight million children with disabilities living in America? It further found that more than half of them were not receiving an adequate education and that more than one million of these children were excluded from the public school system. Thankfully, the laws have changed. Today's laws now specify that all disabled children between the ages of three and twenty-one must have "free appropriate public education" (FAPE). An exception is that if state law exempts a child aged three to five or eighteen to twenty-one, the federal law will not be applied, so FAPE is not applicable.

My experience as a teacher has been that school districts are often not in compliance with special education laws. The school district can be reported to the department of education for this failure. It is not the parents' fault that a district doesn't have an autism specialist, a speech pathologist, or a certified special education (SPED) teacher. It is the school's responsibility to be in compliance. Schools may try to get out of offering services when possible, so it is essential for non-compliance issues to be reported.

Perfect Phrases for Describing Learning Disabilities

When teachers participate in meetings at which a student's learning disability will be discussed, they must be prepared. For instance, they must have read the student's IEP and samples of the student's work. There are two extremes: teachers who have not read the IEP and don't believe in the documents, versus teachers who consider themselves experts in all areas of teaching. There has to be a happy medium, and it is usually the job of the special education director, special education teacher, and guidance counselor to keep the meeting legal and on track. The following phrases might be useful at such a meeting:

It is suspected that your child has dyslexia.

It is suspected that your child may have a learning disability that needs to be tested.

The student does not retain information.

The student feels better after having organized his/her work.

The student has been recommended to participate in a career-pathway program.

The student has difficulty processing out distractions.

The student processes information in a rote manner.

The student questions appropriately for better understanding.

The student quickly adapts to deviations in the lesson.

The student rarely appears overwhelmed or filled with anxiety.

The student shows developmental delays.

Your child appears to be a concrete-sequential learner.

Your child appears to be a kinesthetic learner.

Your child appears to be a visual learner.

Your child appears to be an auditory learner.

Your child appears to have a learning disability.

Your child does not place the needs of others above his/her own.

Your child funnels feedback by . . .

Your child gets bogged down with . . .

Your child has difficulty with public speaking.

Your child has skill-development issues.

Your child hesitates . . .

Your child is a natural-born leader but . . .

Your child needs a structured routine.

Your child practices risk avoidance.

Your child refuses to commit to . . .

Your child requires occupational therapy.

Your child shows a keen ability to multitask.

Your child struggles with . . .

Your child tends to focus on mistakes more than achievements.

Perfect Phrases to Help Advocate for a Child to Receive Special Education Services

Parents and teachers frequently must advocate for children with special needs or learning disabilities. Some parents are unaware of their rights. Teachers should publicly post information specifying where parents can look up their rights in relation to FAPE.

When you begin to speak with a parent, here are some phrases that you can use:

Adaptive learning environments can be made available to your child.

Advocacy and/or legal counsel is available.

As the parent, you must remember that the assessment may include objective tools, such as standardized tests.

As the parent, you must understand that we look at the extent to which the individual can voluntarily and actively . . .

As the parent, you should be aware that in special education disputes, a formal legal proceeding will take place and will be heard by _____ , who will listen to both sides of the dispute and will render a decision based on the state's regulations or statutes.

As the parent, you should be aware that the application of assistive devices and assistive services can be used to enable the individual with disabilities to function better. Insurance in many cases will cover the cost of . . .

As the parent, you should know that this information is confidential. The definition of "education records" has legal significance in terms of the privacy of student records. If you have questions, refer to FERPA.

Before you make any decisions to change schools and send your child to a charter school, please be aware that charter schools are public schools that have been created by a group of teachers, parents, and/or a community-based organization. The schools are usually sponsored by an existing local public school board, county or local board of education, state authority, or university, whereby the sponsoring organization has limited responsibility for oversight of the school. The notion of charter schools is that the schools are exempt from many laws governing public school districts. According to [state] guidelines, in order for these schools to keep their charter, they must demonstrate student achievement, or the charter won't be renewed at the end of the contractual period. This is why we may not recommend that your child switch from his/her IEP program with us to attend a program that may not be able to offer him/her . . .

As you may be aware, a public school district must attempt a _____ plan before changing a student's placement to a more restrictive environment—unless, of course, there is a . . .

Perfect Phrases for Explaining the Special Education Assessment Process to Parents

School districts use a variety of tests to diagnose children in order to determine special education needs. Among the most common tests are the Peabody Picture Vocabulary Test, Peabody Developmental Motor Scale, Stanford-Binet Intelligence Scale, Battelle Developmental Inventory, and Vineland Adaptive Behavior Scale. Parents must give consent before their children can be tested. Before giving consent, they may want to find out from the teacher how the results will be used and what services might be made available to their children. Here are some phrases that you might want to use for these purposes:

We need to test your child for . . .

The test will be administered in the child's native language.

Based on the student's IEP, directions will be administered appropriately.

The student will be allotted time concessions.

_____ is a follow-up from a functional behavioral assessment.

_____ is an evaluation. It can be specific to one problem area academically, or it can include . . .

_____ has been modified to meet the requirements and capabilities of special-needs youngsters.

_____ is used to enable an individual with a disability to function better.

_____ or relevant information will be used to assess the child's ability to screen out distractions and stay on task.

_____ is usually applied to help a student focus on the task at hand.

A behavior-intervention plan should also . . .

A certain amount of articulation difficulty is normal, so we would like to monitor . . .

Abstract concepts require higher-order cognitive processes. Currently, your child is having noticeable difficulties in processing these concepts.

The Adaptive Learning Environment Program allows a student on an IEP to . . .

An educational setting and program for students with learning or behavior disorders in which the environment is adapted or altered to _____ is offered in the following contexts at our institution . . .

At the right level for the chronological age of the child, the child should be able to _____ but currently can only . . .

Attention issues have been noted by . . .

The behavior-intervention plan consists of . . .

Criterion-referenced assessment will be used. Understand that this is a method of assessment in which the individual's score is compared with an established cutoff.

"Exceptional" usually refers to any student whose physical, mental, or behavioral . . .

Perfect Phrases for Placing a Child in Special Education

Here are some phrases that can be used by teachers, as well as parents and administrators, serving as special education advocates:

[child's name] is owed due process under _____ law.

We would like to put your child on a 504. That means [child's name] will receive an individualized plan that will specify what accommodations and services he/she will get from the school in comparison with nondisabled peers.

We would like to put your child on an individualized education plan, or IEP. Under federal and state laws, the following accommodations can be made for your child . . .

When a child's entire educational program, including all related services, is provided in a separate location or special education school, it means that your child is entitled to services that may include . . .

Due-process procedural safeguards are put in place to protect a child's (and the parents') rights in terms of . . .

I understand your concern, but while all states are mandated to provide special education services to students whose scores are substantially lower than the average, not all states mandate services to those who are . . .

If you wish to appeal our decision, you may contact the state's department of education.

In order to comply, we will be using assistive technology.

In order to identify children in need of special education services, our district plans to . . .

"EHA" stands for Education for All Handicapped Children Act; this allows your child . . .

Under the Americans with Disabilities Act (1990), we are required to . . .

Perfect Phrases for Explaining Special Education Options

Many parents have not had educational training and do not understand the options available to them. Opening up the topic that something may make the child different from his or her peers can upset parents. When phrasing special education options, you must be careful in what you suggest and how you suggest it. This is why appropriate and neutral phrasing is necessary. Here are some examples to help you speak with parents of children who you may suspect need to be assessed or have special needs in the classroom:

Assistive device can be used to help your child . . .

Assistive technology is available for your child.

Can I recommend you read the newest research?

Can we discuss the developmental disability?

Can we talk about the developmental delays we have noticed in your child?

Certified occupational therapy can be made available for your child.

Given your child's poor handwriting . . .

If the child does not "outgrow" certain problems, we will test him/her for . . .

If your child has problems with central auditory processing, we can . . .

In general, behavior that enables children to "fit in" with their environment and peers results in _____ ; as it applies to your child, we want to note . . .

In your child's IEP, we have noted an inability to perform coordinated movements, although there isn't any apparent problem in . . .

May we recommend the following special needs advocate: [advocate's name].

Modifications for the child will include . . .

Our district follows one approach, which is to group students in special classes that ignore their diagnoses or educational classification. Instead, it groups them on the basis of the severity of their needs. It is controversial, but it is our policy. If you wish to challenge our policy, contact _____ at the department of education.

Our long-range goals will include . . .

Our strategies emphasize remediation of . . .

Parents should understand what these terms mean. May I take a moment to explain to you the different requirements that local education agencies have regarding a range of settings available to educate students, including the mainstream classroom, regular (mainstream) with push-in services, mainstream with pullout services, self-contained special classes, and homebound instruction.

Sometimes performance deviates from the average. Additional services are sometimes necessary to meet the individual's needs when exceptional students are identified.

Sometimes a central auditory processing disorder will result in a student's . . .

The Department of Social Services offers programs providing financial assistance for needy children whose parents have abandoned them or who are unable to support them.

The _____ descriptor can be applied to materials in order for us to adapt the curriculum to . . .

The level of actual accomplishment or proficiency your child has achieved is . . .

The methods of _____ are suggested, but we need your permission to . . .

The plan is supposed to be based on positive inducements.

The process of focusing has proved difficult for [child's name].

The school is suggesting a behavior-intervention plan.

The student has problems using expressive language.

The student may be eligible for speech and language services.

We are in compliance . . .

We are not in compliance as of yet because . . .

We can attribute . . .

We can offer you a case management service. This is a service usually seen only in cases in which there are many needs or different services or providers requiring coordination and oversight.

We have measured in years, months, and days, as opposed to "mental age."

We have noted social or behavioral functioning . . .

We plan to formalize _____ so that it targets specific behaviors for alteration.

We prefer the word challenged *instead of . . .*

We will automatically accommodate . . .

We will be using observational methods and/or interviews.

We will include any environmental or proactive changes the staff will make in order to . . .

We would like to test your child for attention deficit/ hyperactivity disorder.

Would you mind keeping a log of your activities in relation to your child?

Would you keep a log of your child's food intake and behavioral reactions?

Your child has difficulty with nontangibles such as concepts, ideas, images, and symbols.

Your child has shown difficulty . . .

Perfect Phrases for Discussing Special Education Students with Parents

When you need to discuss a child one-on-one during a parent conference, be sure that you are following the respective IEP and/or 504 plan put in place by the special education department in your school. Some schools do not always comply with these mandates. Teachers may not complete their paperwork or may even be unaware of which students are on plans if the plans have not been shared with the teacher.

By law, information regarding all special education needs of an individual child under your care must be available to you so that you can make the proper adaptations to your lessons. Be careful not to leave any related documents out where they could be read, as that would be a breach of confidentiality and FERPA rules. You should report any violations of privacy to the administration.

Here are some pertinent phrases to use if you must discuss a child's special needs with the parents:

Your child does not have the intellectual ability to understand relationships and to recognize . . .

Your child does not meet eligibility requirements under state law.

Your child suffers from attention deficit/hyperactivity disorder.

Your child doesn't match the abilities of students in the "traditional" environment.

Your child has been diagnosed with dysgraphia.

Your child has been recommended for . . .

Your child has difficulty with abstract reasoning.

Your child has difficulty with concrete items.

Your child has dyslexia.

Your child has dyspraxia.

Your child has emotional and behavioral disorders.

Your child has limited response or adjustment to . . .

Your child has trouble with fine motor skills.

Your child has trouble with gross motor skills.

Your child is eligible for adaptive physical education in order to . . .

Your child is finding the schoolwork difficult and is acting out.

Your child is handicapped. We understand that this is a limitation related to a disability.

Your child is having problems with age-appropriate . . .

Your child is having trouble differentiating between inside and outside voice.

Your child is not behaving in age-appropriate ways.

Your child is not mentally retarded but instead is developmentally disabled in the area of . . .

Your child is suspected of having a behavior disorder.

Your child may be eligible for what is known as an extended school year.

Your child may be removed from the program if _____ is shown.

Your child may have a disability.

Your child may need to meet with . . .

Your child will need to have an aural evaluation.

Your child meets the needs of the . . .

Your child shows significant hearing loss.

Your child shows signs of being emotionally disturbed.

Your child shows signs of mental retardation.

Your child's active range of motion includes . . .

Your child's neurological dysfunctions are causing him/her to . . .

Your child's sensory input or stimulation is . . .

Appendix A

Academic Abbreviations

The most common acronyms and initialisms that all teachers should know are as follows:

ADA: Americans with Disabilities Act
ADD: attention deficit disorder
ADHD: attention deficit/hyperactivity disorder
AFDC: Aid to Families with Dependent Children
AFT: American Federation of Teachers
AIP: academic improvement plan
AP: advanced placement
AYP: adequate yearly progress
CBE: community-based education
CECAS: Comprehensive Exceptional Children Accountability System
CP: cerebral palsy
CRISS: creating independence through student-owned strategies
CST: child study team
CTB: competency testing battery

DD: developmentally delayed
D/HH: deaf/hard of hearing
DSS: Department of Social Services
ED: emotional disturbance
EH: emotionally handicapped
ELL: English-language learner
EMH: educable mentally handicapped
EOC: end-of-course
ESE: elementary and secondary education
ESEA: Elementary and Secondary Education Act
ESL: English as a second language
ESOL: English speakers of other languages
ETR: evaluation team report
ETS: Educational Testing Service
FAPE: Free Appropriate Public Education
FBA: functional behavioral assessment
FERPA: Family Educational Rights and Privacy Act
FRL: free and reduced-priced lunch
GED: general equivalency diploma
IDEA: Individuals with Disabilities Education Act
IEP: individualized education plan
IFSP: individualized family service plan
LEA: local education agency
LEP: limited English proficient
LRE: least-restrictive environment
NAEP: National Assessment of Educational Progress
NCLB: No Child Left Behind
PEP: personalized education plan
PSAT: Pre-Scholastic Assessment Test
PTA: Parent-Teacher Association

PTSA: Parent Teacher Student Association
PTSO: Parent Teacher Student Organization
SAC: school advisory council
SBE: state board of education
SEA: state education agency
SIP: school improvement plan
SPED: special eduation department

Appendix B

Important Contact Information for the Federal Sector

General Education Inquiries

U.S. Department of Education
400 Maryland Avenue SW
Washington, DC 20202
URL contacts page: ed.gov/about/contacts/gen/index.html

FERPA Violations

Family Policy Compliance Office
U.S. Department of Education
400 Maryland Avenue SW
Washington, DC 20202-5920

Civil Rights Violations

U.S. Department of Education
Office for Civil Rights
Customer Service Team
400 Maryland Avenue SW
Washington, DC 20202-1100

Phone: (800) 421-3481
Fax: (202) 245-6840
TDD: (877) 521-2172
E-mail: ocr@ed.gov

American Civil Liberties Union
125 Broad Street, Eighteenth Floor
New York, NY 10004
Website: aclu.org (In the search box, type "school law"
    —cases law can be easily traced.)
ACLU online: aclu.org/contact/general (for contact form)

New England Global Network LLC
P.O. Box 72
Lanesborough, MA 01237
Fax: (413) 442-1221
Website: negn.org

Appendix C

Contacts for Departments of Education for Individual States and U.S. Territories

Alabama

Alabama Department of Education
Gordon Persons Office Building
50 North Ripley Street
P.O. Box 302101
Montgomery, AL 36104-3833
Phone: (334) 242-9700
Fax: (334) 242-9708
E-mail: dmurray@alsde.edu
Website: alsde.edu/html/home.asp

Alaska

Alaska Department of Education and Early Development
801 West Tenth Street, Suite 200
P.O. Box 110500
Juneau, AK 99811-0500
Phone: (907) 465-2800
Fax: (907) 465-4156

TTY: (907) 465-2815
E-mail: dorothy_knuth@eed.state.ak.us or
    webmaster@eed.state.ak.us
Website: eed.state.ak.us

Arizona

Arizona Department of Education
1535 West Jefferson Street
Phoenix, AZ 85007
Phone: (602) 542-4361, (800) 352-4558
Fax: (602) 542-5440
E-mail: adeinbox@ade.az.gov
Website: ade.az.gov

Arkansas

Arkansas Department of Education
Four State Capitol Mall, Room 304A
Little Rock, AR 72201-1071
Phone: (501) 682-4204
Fax: (501) 682-1079
E-mail: ken.james@arkansas.gov
Website: http://arkansased.org

California

California Department of Education
1430 N Street
Sacramento, CA 95814-5901
Phone: (916) 319-0800
Fax: (916) 319-0100
E-mail: joconnell@cde.ca.gov
Website: cde.ca.gov

Colorado

Colorado Department of Education
201 East Colfax Avenue

Denver, CO 80203-1704
Phone: (303) 866-6600
Fax: (303) 830-0793
E-mail: howerter_c@cde.state.co.us
Website: www.cde.state.co.us

Connecticut
Connecticut Department of Education
State Office Building
165 Capitol Avenue
Hartford, CT 06106-1630
Phone: (860) 713-6548, (800) 465-4014
Fax: (860) 713-7017
E-mail: thomas.murphy@po.state.ct.us
Website: state.ct.us/sde

Delaware
Delaware Department of Education
401 Federal Street, Suite 2
Dover, DE 19901-3639
Phone: (302) 735-4000
Fax: (302) 739-4654
Email: mcollier@doe.k12.de.us or vwoodruff@doe.k12.de.us
Website: doe.state.de.us

District of Columbia
District of Columbia Public Schools
825 North Capitol Street NE, Ninth Floor
Washington, DC 20002
Phone: (202) 724-4222
Fax: (202) 442-5026
E-mail: webmaster@k12.dc.us
Website: k12.dc.us/dcps/home.html

Florida
Florida Department of Education
Turlington Building, Suite 1514
325 West Gaines Street
Tallahassee, FL 32399-0400
Phone: (850) 245-0505
Fax: (850) 245-9667
E-mail: annette.deason@fldoe.org or commissioner@fldoe.org
Website: fldoe.org

Georgia
Georgia Department of Education
2066 Twin Towers East
205 Jesse Hill Jr. Drive SE
Atlanta, GA 30334-5001
Phone: (404) 656-2800, (800) 311-3627 (Georgia residents only)
Fax: (404) 651-8737
E-mail: brturner@doe.k12.ga.us or kathycox@doe.k12.ga.us
Website: doe.k12.ga.us/index.asp

Hawaii
Hawaii Department of Education
Systems Accountability Office
1390 Miller Street, Room 411
Honolulu, HI 96813
Phone: (808) 586-3283
Fax: (808) 586-3440
E-mail: robert_mcclelland@notes.k12.hi.us
Website: http://doe.k12.hi.us

Idaho
Idaho Department of Education
Len B. Jordan Office Building
650 West State Street
P.O. Box 83720

Boise, ID 83720-0027
Phone: (208) 332-6800, (800) 432-4601 (Idaho residents only)
Fax: (208) 334-2228
TTY: (800) 377-3529
E-mail: news@sde.state.id.us
Website: sde.state.id.us/dept

Illinois

Illinois State Board of Education
100 North First Street
Springfield, IL 62777
Phone: (217) 782-4321, (866) 262-6663 (Illinois residents only)
Fax: (217) 524-4928
TTY: (217) 782-1900
E-mail: rwatts@isbe.net or statesup@isbe.net
Website: isbe.net

Indiana

Indiana Department of Education
State House, Room 229
Indianapolis, IN 46204-2795
Phone: (317) 232-6610
Fax: (317) 233-6326
E-mail: webmaster@doe.state.in.us
Website: doe.state.in.us

Iowa

Iowa Department of Education
Grimes State Office Building
400 East Fourteenth Street
Des Moines, IA 50319-0146
Phone: (515) 281-3436
Fax: (515) 281-4122
E-mail: kathy.petosa@iowa.gov
Website: state.ia.us/educate

Kansas

Kansas Department of Education
120 South East Tenth Avenue
Topeka, KS 66612-1182
Phone: (785) 296-3201
Fax: (785) 296-7933
TTY: (785) 296-6338
E-mail: bcorkins@ksde.org or lasnider@ksde.org
Website: ksde.org

Kentucky

Kentucky Department of Education
Capital Plaza Tower, First Floor
500 Mero Street
Frankfort, KY 40601
Phone: (502) 564-3421, (800) 533-5372 (Kentucky residents only)
Fax: (502) 564-6470
E-mail: webmaster@education.ky.gov
Website: education.ky.gov

Louisiana

Louisiana Department of Education
1201 North Third
P.O. Box 94064
Baton Rouge, LA 70804-9064
Phone: (225) 342-4411, (877) 453-2721
Fax: (225) 342-0781
E-mail: customerservice@la.gov
Website: louisianaschools.net/lde/index.html

Maine

Maine Department of Education
Burton M. Cross State Office Building
111 Sewall Street
23 State House Station

Augusta, ME 04333-0023
Phone: (207) 624-6600
Fax: (207) 624-6601
TTY: (207) 624-6800
E-mail: tammy.morrill@maine.gov or susan.gendron@maine.gov
Website: maine.gov/portal/education

Maryland

Maryland Department of Education
200 West Baltimore Street
Baltimore, MD 21201
Phone: (410) 767-0100
Fax: (410) 333-6033
E-mail: rpeiffer@msde.state.md.us
Website: marylandpublicschools.org/msde

Massachusetts

Massachusetts Department of Education
350 Main Street
Malden, MA 02148
Phone: (781) 338-3000
Fax: (781) 338-3395
TTY: (800) 439-2370
E-mail: www@doe.mass.edu
Website: doe.mass.edu

Michigan

Michigan Department of Education
608 West Allegan Street
P.O. Box 30008
Lansing, MI 48909
Phone: (517) 373-3324
Fax: (517) 335-4565
E-mail: marlows@michigan.gov or mde-supt@michigan.gov
Website: michigan.gov/mde

Minnesota

Minnesota Department of Education
1500 Highway 36 West
Roseville, MN 55113-4266
Phone: (651) 582-8200
Fax: (651) 582-8727
TTY: (651) 582-8201
E-mail: mde.commissioner@state.mn.us or alice.seagren@state
    .mn.us
Website: http://education.state.mn.us/mde/index.html

Mississippi

Mississippi Department of Education
Central High School
359 North West Street
P.O. Box 771
Jackson, MS 39205
Phone: (601) 359-3513
Fax: (601) 359-3242
E-mail: cblanton@mde.k12.ms.us
Website: mde.k12.ms.us

Missouri

Missouri Department of Elementary and Secondary Education
205 Jefferson Street
P.O. Box 480
Jefferson City, MO 65102-0480
Phone: (573) 751-4212
Fax: (573) 751-8613
TTY: (800) 735-2966
E-mail: pubinfo@dese.mo.gov
Website: http://dese.mo.gov

Montana
Montana Office of Public Instruction
P.O. Box 202501
Helena, MT 59620-2501
Phone: (406) 444-2082, (888) 231-9393 (Montana residents only)
Fax: (406) 444-3924
E-mail: cbergeron@mt.gov
Website: opi.mt.gov

Nebraska
Nebraska Department of Education
301 Centennial Mall South
P.O. Box 94987
Lincoln, NE 68509-4987
Phone: (402) 471-2295
Fax: (402) 471-0117
TTY: (402) 471-7295
Email: john.clark@nde.ne.gov or jodi.sommers@nde.ne.gov
Website: nde.state.ne.us

Nevada
Nevada Department of Education
700 East Fifth Street
Carson City, NV 89701
Phone: (775) 687-9217
Fax: (775) 687-9101
E-mail: darnold@doe.nv.gov
Website: doe.nv.gov

New Hampshire
New Hampshire Department of Education
Hugh J. Gallan State Office Park
101 Pleasant Street
Concord, NH 03301

Phone: (603) 271-3495, (800) 339-9900
Fax: (603) 271-1953
TTY: Relay NH 711
E-mail: lkincaid@ed.state.nh.us
Website: ed.state.nh.us

New Jersey
New Jersey Department of Education
100 Riverview Plaza
P.O. Box 500
Trenton, NJ 08625-0500
Phone: (609) 292-4469
Fax: (609) 777-4099
Website: state.nj.us/education

New Mexico
New Mexico Public Education Department
300 Don Gaspar
Santa Fe, NM 87501-2786
Phone: (505) 827-7889
Fax: (505) 827-6588
E-mail: rwilliams@ped.state.nm.us or jgallegos@ped.state.nm.us
Website: ped.state.nm.us

New York
New York State Education Department
Education Building, Room 111
89 Washington Avenue
Albany, NY 12234
Phone: (518) 474-5844
Fax: (518) 473-4909
E-mail: rmills@mail.nysed.gov
Website: nysed.gov

North Carolina

Department of Public Instruction
301 North Wilmington Street
Raleigh, NC 27601
Phone: (919) 807-3300
Fax: (919) 807-3445
E-mail: information@dpi.state.nc.us
Website: ncpublicschools.org

North Dakota

North Dakota Department of Public Instruction
Department 201
600 East Boulevard Avenue
Bismarck, ND 58505-0440
Phone: (701) 328-2260
Fax: (701) 328-2461
E-mail: lnorbeck@nd.gov or wsanstead@nd.gov
Website: dpi.state.nd.us

Ohio

Ohio Department of Education
25 South Front Street
Columbus, OH 43215-4183
Phone: (614) 466 4839, (877) 644-6338
Fax: (614) 728 9300
TTY: (888) 886-0181
E-mail: patti.grey@ode.state.oh.us or susan.zelman@ode.state
    .oh.us
Website: ode.state.oh.us

Oklahoma

Oklahoma State Department of Education
2500 North Lincoln Boulevard
Oklahoma City, OK 73105-4599

Phone: (405) 521-3301
Fax: (405) 521-6205
E-mail: sandy_garrett@sde.state.ok.us
Website: http://sde.state.ok.us

Oregon
Oregon Department of Education
255 Capitol Street NE
Salem, OR 97310-0203
Phone: (503) 947-5600
Fax: (503) 378-5156
TTY: (503) 378-2892
E-mail: gene.evans@state.or.us
Website: ode.state.or.us

Pennsylvania
Pennsylvania Department of Education
333 Market Street
Harrisburg, PA 17126-0333
Phone: (717) 787-5820
Fax: (717) 787-7222
TTY: (717) 783-8445
E-mail: 00admin@state.pa.us
Website: pde.state.pa.us

Rhode Island
Rhode Island Department of Elementary and Secondary Education
255 Westminster Street
Providence, RI 02903-3400
Phone: (401) 222-4600
Fax: (401) 222-2537
TTY: (800) 745-5555
E-mail: ride0777@ride.ri.gov
Website: ridoe.net

South Carolina

South Carolina Department of Education
1006 Rutledge Building
1429 Senate Street
Columbia, SC 29201
Phone: (803) 734-8493
Fax: (803) 734-3389
E-mail: mlint@sde.state.sc.us or info@sde.state.sc.us
Website: myscschools.com

South Dakota

Department of Education
700 Governors Drive
Pierre, SD 57501-2291
Phone: (605) 773-3553
Fax: (605) 773-6139
TTY: (605) 773-6302
E-mail: melody.schopp@state.sd.us or pam.hoepfer@state.sd.us
Website: http://doe.sd.gov

Tennessee

Tennessee State Department of Education
Andrew Johnson Tower, Sixth Floor
710 James Robertson Parkway
Nashville, TN 37243-0375
Phone: (615) 741-2731
Fax: (615) 532-4791
E-mail: education.comments@state.tn.us
Website: state.tn.us/education

Texas

Texas Education Agency
William B. Travis Building
1701 North Congress Avenue
Austin, TX 78701-1494

Phone: (512) 463-9734
Fax: (512) 463-9838
TTY: (512) 475-3540
E-mail: teainfo@tea.state.tx.us
Website: tea.state.tx.us

Utah

Utah State Office of Education
250 East 500 South
P.O. Box 144200
Salt Lake City, UT 84114-4200
Phone: (801) 538-7500
Fax: (801) 538-7521
E-mail: mark.peterson@schools.utah.gov
Website: schools.utah.gov

Vermont

Vermont Department of Education
120 State Street
Montpelier, VT 05620-2501
Phone: (802) 828-3135
Fax: (802) 828-3140
TTY: (802) 828-2755
E-mail: edinfo@education.state.vt.us
Website: education.vermont.gov

Virginia

Virginia Department of Education
James Monroe Building
101 North Fourteenth Street
P.O. Box 2120
Richmond, VA 23218-2120
Phone: (804) 225-2420
E-mail: charles.pyle@doe.virginia.gov
Website: doe.virginia.gov

Washington

Office of Superintendent of Public Instruction
Old Capitol Building
600 South Washington
P.O. Box 47200
Olympia, WA 98504-7200
Phone: (360) 725-6000
Fax: (360) 753-6712
TTY: (360) 664-3631
E-mail: kconway@ospi.wednet.edu
Website: k12.wa.us

West Virginia

West Virginia Department of Education
Building 6, Room 358
1900 Kanawha Boulevard East
Charleston, WV 25305-0330
Phone: (304) 558-2681
Fax: (304) 558-0048
E-mail: dvermill@access.k12.wv.us
Website: http://wvde.state.wv.us

Wisconsin

Department of Public Instruction
125 South Webster Street
P.O. Box 7841
Madison, WI 53707-7841
Phone: (608) 266-3108, (800) 441-4563
Fax: (608) 266-2529
TTY: (608) 267-2427
E-mail: kay.ihlenfeldt@dpi.state.wi.us
Website: dpi.state.wi.us

Wyoming

Wyoming Department of Education
Hathaway Building, Second Floor
2300 Capitol Avenue
Cheyenne, WY 82002-0050
Phone: (307) 777-7675
Fax: (307) 777-6234
TTY: (307) 777-8546
E-mail: supt@educ.state.wy.us
Website: k12.wy.us

Guam

Guam Public School System
P.O. Box DE
Hagåtña, GU 96932
Phone: (671) 475-0462
Fax: (671) 472-5003
E-mail: lreyes@gdoe.net or tcruz@gdoe.net
Website: gdoe.net

Puerto Rico

Puerto Rico Department of Education
P.O. Box 190759
San Juan, PR 00919-0759
Phone: (787) 759-2000
Fax: (787) 250-0275

Virgin Islands

Virgin Islands Department of Education
44-46 Kongens Gade
Charlotte Amalie, VI 00802
Phone: (340) 774-2810
Fax: (340) 779-7153
Website: doe.vi

The Right Phrase for Every Situation...Every Time

Perfect Phrases for Building Strong Teams
Perfect Phrases for Business Letters
Perfect Phrases for Business Proposals and Business Plans
Perfect Phrases for Business School Acceptance
Perfect Phrases for College Application Essays
Perfect Phrases for Cover Letters
Perfect Phrases for Customer Service
Perfect Phrases for Dealing with Difficult People
Perfect Phrases for Dealing with Difficult Situations at Work
Perfect Phrases for Documenting Employee Performance Problems
Perfect Phrases for Executive Presentations
Perfect Phrases for Landlords and Property Managers
Perfect Phrases for Law School Acceptance
Perfect Phrases for Lead Generation
Perfect Phrases for Managers and Supervisors
Perfect Phrases for Managing Your Small Business
Perfect Phrases for Medical School Acceptance
Perfect Phrases for Meetings
Perfect Phrases for Motivating and Rewarding Employees
Perfect Phrases for Negotiating Salary & Job Offers
Perfect Phrases for Perfect Hiring
Perfect Phrases for the Perfect Interview
Perfect Phrases for Performance Reviews
Perfect Phrases for Real Estate Agents & Brokers
Perfect Phrases for Resumes
Perfect Phrases for Sales and Marketing Copy
Perfect Phrases for the Sales Call
Perfect Phrases for Setting Performance Goals
Perfect Phrases for Small Business Owners
Perfect Phrases for the TOEFL Speaking and Writing Sections
Perfect Phrases for Writing Grant Proposals
Perfect Phrases in American Sign Language for Beginners
Perfect Phrases in French for Confident Travel
Perfect Phrases in German for Confident Travel
Perfect Phrases in Italian for Confident Travel
Perfect Phrases in Spanish for Confident Travel to Mexico
Perfect Phrases in Spanish for Construction
Perfect Phrases in Spanish for Gardening and Landscaping
Perfect Phrases in Spanish for Household Maintenance and Child Care
Perfect Phrases in Spanish for Restaurant and Hotel Industries

Visit mhprofessional.com/perfectphrases for a complete product listing.

Learn more. Do more.

THE IDEAL PERFORMANCE SUPPORT SOLUTION FOR MANAGERS AND SUPERVISORS

With over 30,000 phrases, *Perfect Phrases for Managers* is an unmatched digital resource that provides managers at every level with the skills they need to effectively manage any situation.

From performance reviews to documenting problems, to motivating and coaching teams, to managing difficult people and embarrassing situations, this performance support tool will help your company create an environment for exceptional performance.

Go to **www.perfectphrases.com** to learn more about *Perfect Phrases for Managers* and how you can access:

- A "Things to Consider" section with hundreds of bite-size coaching tips
- Audio clips from actual conversations
- Strategies for opening up healthy communication

The right phrase for every situation, every time.

Visit www.perfectphrases.com to learn how your company can qualify for a trial subscription.